Praise for *Moses*

"Adam Hamilton is a compelling storyteller. As in so much of his celebrated ministry, here he provides ready access to the riches of faith. In retelling this foundational narrative, he weaves into his account his own experience of the 'geography of Moses.' Readers will find this book a helpful entry point into a story that makes welcome linkage between faith and historical reality."
—**Walter Brueggemann**, Columbia Theological Seminary, author of *The Prophetic Imagination*

"I'm always challenged, consistently inspired, and occasionally rocked by Adam Hamilton's leadership and teaching. His work on Moses challenges assumptions and prompts GOD-honoring action. Get it. Read it. Act on it."
—**Mark Beeson**, Founding Pastor of Granger Community Church, Granger, IN

"My congregation loves the way Adam Hamilton's books connect the Scriptures with our modern context. I'm excited to share with them his latest work, Moses, and take them on a journey from Egypt through Sinai and on to the Promised Land."
—**Katie Z. Dawson**, Lead Pastor of Immanuel UMC, Des Moines, author of *All Earth Is Waiting*

"Some books on Moses are strictly academic; others are strictly devotional. In his trademark style, Adam Hamilton finds the best of both options and offers a centered portrayal of this extraordinary hero of the faith. There are so many rich insights in this book that it is best savored, not devoured, in the company of others. Just like manna from heaven."
-**Magrey R. deVega**, Senior Pastor of Hyde Park UMC, Tampa, author of *Awaiting the Already*

"Adam Hamilton gives an insightful, compelling portrait of Moses. Based on sound biblical scholarship, he vividly describes the character of Moses, his life and times, his importance in the Hebrew Scriptures, and his profound significance for Christian faith."
—**Harold C. Washington**, Professor of Hebrew Bible, Saint Paul School of Theology

"Join Adam Hamilton as your tour guide in tracing the life story of Moses. Along the journey, Hamilton relates his first-hand experience visiting sites in Egypt and Jordan. The result is a pilgrimage experience, enriched with reflection on the meaning of Torah for the original authors and for contemporary Christians."
—**Thomas B. Dozeman**, United Theological Seminary, author of *Commentary on Exodus*

"Adam Hamilton has the remarkable gift of taking sometimes complex and extensive resources and making them both approachable and applicable. In his latest work, Moses, Hamilton uses the powerful tool of narrative to help us engage more deeply a story that many of us think of as familiar."
—**Sarah Heath**, Lead Pastor of First UMC, Costa Mesa, CA, author of *What's Your Story?*

"Once again, Adam Hamilton shows he's a master teacher who guides his audience into lively conversation and deep thinking. His book Moses is a model of what it means to focus on the Bible's bold content with honesty and faithfulness. This is Bible study as it should be."
—**Matthew R. Schlimm**, University of Dubuque Theological Seminary, author of *From Fratricide to Forgiveness*

ADAM HAMILTON

MOSES

In the Footsteps of the
RELUCTANT PROPHET

Abingdon Press / Nashville

Moses
In the Footsteps of the Reluctant Prophet

Copyright © 2017 Abingdon Press
All rights reserved.

This book is printed on elemental chlorine-free paper.
Library of Congress Cataloging-in-Publication Data has been requested.

978-1-5018-0788-6

17 18 19 20 21 22 23 24 25 26—10 9 8 7 6 5 4 3 2 1
MANUFACTURED IN THE UNITED STATES OF AMERICA

To John Ed Mathison, one of the Jethros in my life,

and James Ridgeway, who made it possible
for me to walk in the footsteps of Moses

CONTENTS

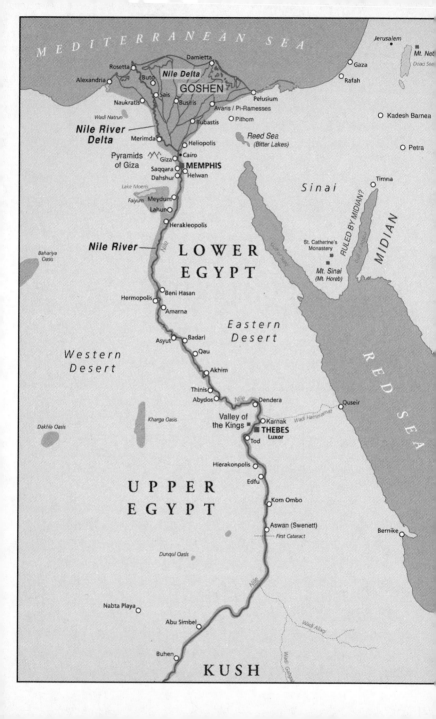

INTRODUCTION

Moses.

He is the single most important figure in the Hebrew Bible (the Christian Old Testament). His presence is felt throughout the Christian New Testament. The epic account of his life, together with the deliverance of the Israelite slaves from bondage in Egypt, is the defining story of the Jewish people. The Jewish festivals of Sukkot (Tabernacles), Shavuot (Weeks), and Passover, as well as the holy days of Rosh Hashanah (New Year) and Yom Kippur (Day of Atonement), are rooted in Moses' story and the Law attributed to him, as is the weekly observance of the Sabbath among Jews.

For Christians, Moses' life serves as the backdrop for much that is found in the Gospels, including the story of Jesus' flight to Egypt, the Sermon on the Mount, many of Jesus' sayings in the Gospel of John, the activities of Jesus around Jerusalem, the Last Supper, and the Crucifixion. In the Gospel account of Christ's transfiguration, Moses actually appears to Jesus and speaks to him. Moses is mentioned by name more than seventy times in the New Testament, and his life, story, and commands are alluded to in nearly every New Testament book.

Throughout history, his story has continued to speak to each successive generation. American slaves composed songs about Moses as they yearned for freedom. Moses is enshrined in the architecture of the U.S. Supreme Court—inside on the south frieze as one of the great lawgivers of history and outside on the eastern pediment. Dr. Martin Luther King Jr., in his final sermon delivered the night before his death, drew upon the story of Moses ascending Mount Nebo. King proclaimed that he had "been to the mountaintop," where, like Moses, he claimed to have seen the Promised Land.[1] Moses' story has been captured in art, music, literature, and film.

The account of Moses and the Exodus was originally passed down from generation to generation orally since most Israelites at that time could not read or write. Instead they told stories—stories intended to entertain, to shape the identity of a people, and to teach them about God and God's will for humankind. We often read these stories with a certain seriousness, but for centuries they were told around campfires after supper or to children before they were put to bed. The stories contain heroes and villains, suspense and intrigue, and no small amount of humor.

Among the many things I appreciate about Moses' story is what an unlikely hero he was. He was a Hebrew adopted into Pharaoh's family. He was a murderer and fugitive from the law. He was an elderly sheepherder from the desert whom God called to deliver the Israelites. He appears to have had some kind of speech impediment, yet became Israel's greatest prophet. And, as we will see in every chapter of this book, he was imperfect, afraid, reluctant, and often frustrated, all of which makes him so very human. Yet, despite all of this, the Book of Deuteronomy closes with these words: "No prophet like Moses has yet emerged in Israel; Moses knew the LORD face-to-face!" (Deuteronomy 34:10).

Walking in the Footsteps of Moses, But Where Exactly Did He Walk?

In preparation for writing this book, I traveled to Egypt with a film crew to see the places associated with Moses and the Exodus. I wanted to walk in the footsteps of Moses and become familiar with the geographical setting for his story. We were blessed to have several outstanding Egyptologists, archaeologists, and guides to help us explore the land.

In this book I'll intersperse travel descriptions with historical, archaeological, and scriptural information in a way that I hope will make Egypt vivid and bring the story of Moses to life. On the DVD that is available with this book, I take viewers to each of the key locations associated with Moses' story. I've included maps, photographs, and illustrations of many of these places throughout the book.

On the map of Egypt at the beginning of this introduction, you can see places associated with Moses and the Exodus. Since few of these places are actually named in the story of Moses, students of Moses' life are left to speculate. Accuracy regarding where the events took place is not essential to reading and understanding the story, but anchoring the stories geographically does make them a bit more interesting.

Current-day Mount Sinai, also known as Mount Horeb or Jebel Musa ("the Mountain of Moses")

I've suggested that Moses was born and raised in the ancient city of Thebes (modern Luxor), though he could have been born in Memphis or possibly in the Nile River Delta; a case could be made for each of these three locations. I've assumed, as most do, that Moses' confrontations with the pharaoh occurred in the city of Pi-Ramesses (or simply Ramesses, which is sometimes spelled as Ramses or Rameses) and that the parting of the Red Sea actually took place at the "Reed Sea," which may have been the Bitter Lakes or another lake not far from there. The biblical Mount Sinai may or may not have been the current-day Mount Sinai; people have claimed at least twelve locations as being the Mount Sinai of Moses, though the one I'll mention in the text has been visited by pilgrims for over 1,700 years. While in Egypt, we visited most of these sites, before ending our journey at Mount Nebo in Jordan.

It has been said that the Holy Land is the fifth Gospel; those who visit there never read the Gospels the same way again. I'd suggest that the land of Egypt, including the Sinai, functions as a sixth book of the Pentateuch; visiting the archaeological sites and traversing its geography can lead to a fresh and insightful reading of Moses and the story of the Exodus.

About This Book

I want to say up front that this book is not intended to be a complete biography of Moses, nor a verse-by-verse exposition of his life as found in Exodus–Deuteronomy. I'll cover only the highlights of Moses' story, leaving many important details on the proverbial cutting room floor in order to focus on other parts of the narrative. Neither is this book intended as a scholarly commentary on Moses, though I've read many such books as I researched this volume. (I've listed some of my favorite commentaries in the back of this book, under the heading "For Further Reading.")

Instead, I hope this book will not only help readers come to know Moses, but see how his life and story speak to our lives and stories today. Moses' story is an important part of sacred Scripture; as such, Jews and Christians believe it reveals something to us about God, about ourselves, and about God's will for our lives.

Did Moses Write His Own Story?

The story of Moses, from his birth to his death and the amazing adventures in between, is found in four of the first five books of the Bible. It begins in Exodus, continues through Leviticus and Numbers, and concludes with the final verses of Deuteronomy. The first five books of the Bible are referred to as the Torah, the Pentateuch, the Books of Moses, the Law, or simply "Moses." Tradition ascribes the authorship of these first five books to Moses, though most mainline scholars suggest that while Moses may have written portions of these books, most of his story was passed down orally for generations long before it was written down.

This makes sense as you read the Torah. The Torah doesn't name its author, though Moses is the central character of four of the five books. Moses is usually described in the third person. Things are said about him that he would likely not have said about himself. (For instance, Numbers 12:3 notes, "Now the man Moses was humble, more so than anyone on earth." If Moses wrote those words, then he was *not* the most humble man on earth!) Some statements in the Torah seem to come from a time much later than that of Moses. Deuteronomy ends with Moses' death, a passage that clearly was written by someone else. In the Torah there are multiple stories where it appears that material from various sources has been edited together. The Exodus story as it is told in Deuteronomy is different in some details from the version told in Books of Exodus, Leviticus, and Numbers. For these reasons and more, most mainline scholars today believe that the Torah was drawn from multiple sources, written and edited over a period of centuries.[2]

Having said that, we can note that the Torah does include verses indicating that Moses wrote some things down, such as Deuteronomy 31:9: "Then Moses wrote this Instruction down and gave it to the priests—the Levites who carry the chest containing the LORD's covenant—and to all of the Israelite elders." The phrase "this

Instruction" appears to refer back to a portion of what is recorded in Deuteronomy. Likewise Exodus 24:4 notes, "Moses then wrote down all the LORD's words." The phrase "all the LORD's words" probably refers to the Ten Commandments and other laws found in Exodus 20–24, or it might include other statements attributed to God beginning in Exodus 3.

Many conservative Christians as well as Orthodox and ultra-Orthodox Jews continue to make the case that Moses was the author of nearly all the Pentateuch or Torah. You can find plenty of articles online making the case for Mosaic authorship of the Torah and offering what the writers consider a convincing case debunking any views to the contrary. On the other hand, you would be hard pressed to find a mainline Christian or a Conservative or Reformed Jewish scholar who did not embrace some form of a composite theory about the authorship of the Pentateuch.

I mention this ongoing question about the Torah's authorship because I think it's useful for those studying Moses to be aware of the conversation. Also, I find the composite view helpful in reading the story of Moses, particularly in places where the timeline seems out of sync or where various accounts of the story seem in conflict.

Was There Really a Moses?

I was invited to a Passover Seder at the home of a rabbi friend, where one of his congregation members said to me, "I am not sure I believe that Moses really existed. There is no archaeological evidence for Moses or that the Israelites were ever enslaved in Egypt. And I don't think it really matters." I was a bit surprised by the comment, coming from a Jewish man at a Passover Seder, but I was not unfamiliar with the argument. The man was referring to the underlying question of "historicity" regarding the biblical narratives: Do they describe actual historical events, and, if so, how historically accurate are their descriptions of people and events?

There are three basic approaches taken by scholars today to the historicity of Moses' story (as well as most of the other stories found in the Pentateuch, Joshua, Judges, and, for some scholars, First and Second Samuel and First and Second Kings). The three approaches are the minimalist, the maximalist, and a position between the two.

Scholars taking the "minimalist" approach tend to read the biblical accounts of Moses (and most other biblical figures prior to the time of Solomon, if not later) as legendary. In their view, these early biblical characters and stories are understood to be, for the ancient Israelites, what myths were for the ancient Greeks— stories that entertained even as they shaped values, religious beliefs, and cultural identity. Minimalist scholars contend that whether Moses really existed is not the point and that the value of his story is not dependent upon its being historically true, anymore than the value of Homer's *Iliad* or *Odyssey* is dependent upon whether Achilles and Odysseus were real people who actually did what was recorded in these epic poems. Was there really a Moses? Possibly, some minimalists would say. Unlikely, other minimalists would answer. Neither group, however, would claim that most of the events described in Exodus–Deuteronomy are historically accurate. This was the view of the Jewish man I met at my friend's Passover Seder.

A second view, and nearly the opposite of the minimalist, is referred to as the "maximalist" approach. (The term, like *minimalist*, was originally used derisively by those who opposed these respective views.) Maximalists see the biblical accounts from Abraham to Solomon as largely or entirely historically accurate. As with minimalists, maximalists hold a range of views, with extreme maximalists maintaining that the story of Moses is historically accurate in every detail, capturing precisely what "really happened."

A third approach, and one held by many mainline and some evangelical Christian scholars, as well as most Conservative and Reform scholars in Judaism, is somewhere between the extreme maximalist and the minimalist positions. Like the others, it encompasses a range of views but generally holds that the authors and editors of the Torah were writing about an actual historical figure named Moses who did in fact lead the Israelites out of slavery in Egypt. But the story is more like an excellent film "based upon actual events" than a documentary intended to convey historical events as accurately as possible. The director and screenwriter of the former have a bit more latitude to tell the story in a way that is both entertaining and inspiring, while still depicting actual events and people. That's how many read the story of Moses and the Exodus.[3]

According to this last view, the biblical authors were not writing as journalists or reporters or even historians. Instead they were writing as master storytellers whose intent was to convey the Israelites' epic and defining story and to reveal the God who claimed Israel as his own. The stories entertained, but more importantly they taught theology, morality, and spirituality. They were read, and continue to be read, not simply to learn about a historical figure named Moses but to learn something about ourselves and about God.

In fact, that is my intention in writing this book about Moses—not simply to summarize Moses' story, but to consider what his story teaches us about ourselves and about God.

When Did Moses Live?

If one believes, as I do, that there was a "historical" Moses, the next question is, When did Moses live? The answer to that question involves determining who the pharaoh of the Exodus was and when the Exodus occurred. On this question there is ongoing debate. The Torah itself does not tell us when Moses lived, the name of the pharaoh whom Moses confronted, nor the timing of the Exodus. There are two dating schemes that are most commonly assigned to the story of Moses.

One dating scheme is based on 1 Kings 6:1, which tells us that Solomon built the Temple in Jerusalem in the fourth year of his reign, and it also tells us that this occurred in the 480th year after the Israelites left Egypt. Solomon is widely thought to have dedicated the Temple in 966 B.C., which would place the Exodus in 1446 B.C. Moses was eighty years old when the Exodus occurred (Exodus 7:7), which would mean he was born in 1526 B.C. This is the common early dating for Moses, and you can find lots of supporting arguments for these dates online, particularly from conservative Christians.

Many believe there is more historical and archaeological support for the Exodus occurring in the thirteenth century B.C., and so a second dating scheme places the Exodus sometime between 1280 and 1260. Exodus 1:11 mentions that the Israelite slaves were forced to build supply cities called "Pithom" and "Rameses." The latter likely refers to the capital city Pi-Ramesses, named after Pharaoh Ramesses II who built it in the 1200s. The city became the northern capital of Egypt at this time. You can read more supporting evidence online for an Exodus during the thirteenth century B.C. Many evangelical and most mainline scholars place the Exodus in this time period and view Ramesses II as the pharaoh of the plagues and the Exodus. Ramesses II conducted massive building campaigns throughout Egypt during his reign. The many statues and temples dedicated to him throughout Egypt, more than to any other pharaoh, likely bear testimony to his own ego.

If we choose a thirteenth-century B.C. date for the Exodus, then Moses was born in the 1300s B.C. But if this is the case, how do we make sense of the note in 1 Kings 6:1 about the Temple being built 480 years after the Israelites were released from slavery in Egypt? Many view the dates given at many points in the Old Testament as more symbolic than chronologic. A generation was generally seen as forty years. Twelve was an important number in Scripture, and the 480 years may simply have been derived from the idea of twelve generations, not a literal 480 years. Even the age of Moses at key intervals of his life, forty years old when he fled Egypt, eighty years old when he was called by God at the burning bush, and 120 years old when he died, are likely rounded numbers with symbolic value.

We can't know for certain when the Exodus occurred. Ultimately it matters little as we read Moses' story and try to understand how it speaks to our lives today. I've assumed throughout this book that Ramesses II was the pharaoh of the Exodus and that the Exodus occurred in the thirteenth century B.C. I did so because this seems to fit better with the archaeological evidence, and because Ramesses II was such a prolific builder with a seemingly oversized ego that he makes a great villain in the story and gives us so many places and structures in Egypt to visit from his period.

With all of this as background, we're ready to begin our study of Moses, the reluctant prophet.

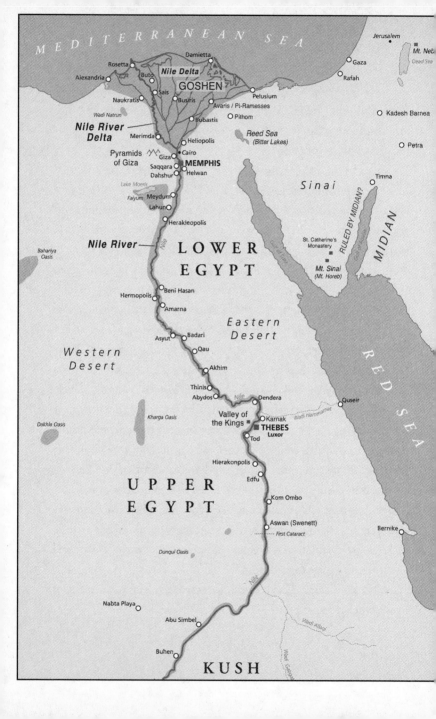

1.

THE BIRTH OF MOSES

We arrived at Cairo International Airport just after nightfall. Though weary from a day of flying, we were excited to finally set foot on Egyptian soil and to catch a glimpse, by night, of the Great Pyramid of Giza. It took an hour and fifteen minutes to drive from the airport, on the northeast side of Cairo, to Giza, a southern suburb of the city. Even at night the streets were congested with the swelling population of twenty million people who live in greater Cairo.

Upon checking into my hotel room, I opened the sliding door to my balcony, and stood for a moment, in awe, as I looked across at the pyramids by night. I was gazing upon the same pyramids that pharaohs, patriarchs, and emperors throughout history had stood before. It was a breathtaking sight.

The Pyramids and the Power of the Pharaohs

Some mistakenly assume that these pyramids were built by the Israelite slaves whom Moses would lead to freedom, but the pyramids were already ancient when Israel was born. They had been standing for at least a thousand years by the time Moses came on the scene.

So, if the Israelites were not involved in the building of these structures, why would we begin our journey—and this book—with the pyramids? One reason is simply that you should never visit Egypt without seeing the pyramids. More importantly, though, we begin with the pyramids because they help us understand the pharaohs and the role they played in Egyptian society. The larger-than-life, semidivine status of the pharaohs, captured in the building of the pyramids, helps us understand the villains or antagonists in Moses' story.

Sometime around 3000 B.C., when the kings or pharaohs first unified Upper and Lower Egypt, a city was built on the west bank of the Nile about thirteen miles south of modern Cairo. This city, located on the boundary of Upper and Lower Egypt, would serve as the new capital of the unified kingdom. We know the city as Memphis. Just north of this ancient capital, and stretching north for miles along the plateau that separates the desert from the Nile, the city's necropolis—its burial ground—was built.

It was there, around 2560 B.C., that a king named Khufu built an enormous burial chamber for himself, a monument to his greatness, in the shape of a pyramid. For almost four millennia this pyramid remained the tallest man-made structure on earth, at 481 feet. It is the only one of the Seven Wonders of the Ancient World still standing. The pyramid of Khufu, known as the Great Pyramid of

Pyramids of Giza, with the city of Giza in the background

Giza, along with the pyramid of his son Khafre and its adjacent sphinx and the pyramid of his grandson Menkaure, together make up the most prominent of the pyramids at Giza.

Over one hundred pyramids have been unearthed in the sands of Egypt, and likely others have yet to be found. It is thought that the pyramids of Giza were built by a workforce of as many as twenty thousand people, most of whom were farmers who worked to construct the pyramids during the seasons when the Nile flooded and they were unable to farm (though some who labored may have been slaves). These massive building projects were possible during periods of economic prosperity and peace. As economic prosperity decreased, so did the size of the pyramids.

Some have described the pyramids as "resurrection machines" intended to ensure that the pharaohs or others buried in them

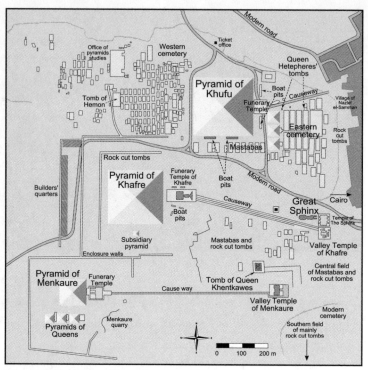

Map of the Giza pyramid complex

completed their journey to the afterlife.[1] Ultimately the pyramids served as an enduring testimony to the power and greatness of the pharaoh whose remains they held.

We traveled to the Giza pyramid complex the day after we arrived in Egypt. As I gazed up at the Great Pyramid, in awe of the massive stones that were so expertly fit together, I wondered how Abraham, Jacob, and even Moses felt as they stood before this very pyramid. We live in a time with magnificent buildings, many of which are taller than these structures, and yet the pyramids still amaze us. The

Standing on the stones of the Great Pyramid gives a sense of the pyramids' size and scale.

pyramids were meant to inspire awe and admiration for the pharaohs who built them. To those searching for Moses in Egypt, the pyramids stand as a silent witness to the power of the ancient pharaohs, and to the Egyptian belief in the pharaohs' semidivine nature that went back a thousand years before the birth of Moses but was still believed about the pharaohs in his day.

From Giza to Luxor

Memphis was the capital of Egypt in the period known by scholars as the Old Kingdom. For most of the New Kingdom, the time in which Moses was born, it wasn't Memphis but Thebes that served as the home of the royal family. Thebes was located about 300 miles south of Memphis, a distance that today takes about an hour by plane.

As noted in the introduction, we cannot be sure when Moses lived. The two most common dating schemes have Moses living from approximately 1526 to 1406 B.C. or from approximately 1350 to 1230 B.C. The latter dating, give or take a decade or two, is more common among mainline scholars, the former among more conservative scholars, though you can find exceptions to this rule. For either of these likely dates of Moses' birth, the Egyptian capital was in Thebes.[2]

I had always assumed that Moses was born in the Nile River Delta—the biblical "Land of Goshen," where the Israelites settled in the time of the patriarch Joseph. Moses' story in Exodus seems, at first glance, to suggest that all Hebrews or Israelites lived in the same general area, and the story seems centered there. Yet during neither of the proposed dates for Moses' birth was there likely a royal palace in the Delta region.[3] However, it is likely that there were Israelite slaves located across Egypt, even if a majority continued to dwell in the Land of Goshen. Hence, it seems plausible or even likely that Moses was born near Thebes, was adopted there by one of the pharaoh's daughters, and lived there for much of his life to the age of forty.[4]

Our journey to walk in the footsteps of Moses took us from Giza, in the southern suburbs of Cairo, to Luxor, the modern name for the ancient city of Thebes. Luxor is a city of roughly five hundred thousand people on the eastern bank of the Nile River. The archaeological remains of the ancient capital of Thebes are intertwined with the modern city of Luxor, lying beneath the modern city in places and yet magnificently exposed in the temples of Luxor and Karnak, which bear witness to the grandeur of this ancient capital. And three miles to the west by northwest of the city, where the Nile River Valley meets the desert plateau, is the famous Valley of the Kings—the necropolis or burial ground of Egypt's kings who reigned from the sixteenth to the eleventh centuries before Christ.

We've been considering historical questions and archaeological sites up to this point, but let's shift our focus to Moses himself and the meaning of his story. My hope is to have his story speak as Scripture—to recount the events of Moses' life, yes, but to ask: What does the story teach us about God, about humanity, and about ourselves? At each point in our account of Moses' life, we will see if we can find ourselves in the story. In this chapter we'll focus on the stories surrounding Moses' birth, as described in the first two chapters of Exodus.

The Terrible Power of Fear

> Now Joseph and all his brothers and all that generation died, but the Israelites were exceedingly fruitful; they multiplied greatly, increased in numbers and became so numerous that the land was filled with them. Then a new king, to whom Joseph meant nothing, came to power in Egypt.
>
> (Exodus 1:6-8 NIV)

As seen in this Scripture, the backdrop for the story of Moses is the story of Joseph, the son of Israel, who was sold by his brothers into slavery and eventually became Pharaoh's second-in-command over Egypt. The story is a masterpiece of ancient literature and is known by many who have never picked up a Bible because of the wonderful way Tim Rice and Andrew Lloyd Webber retold it in the hit Broadway musical *Joseph and the Amazing Technicolor Dreamcoat*.

The biblical story actually fits well a period in Egypt's history in which foreign people, known as Hyksos, settled in the Nile River Delta. These foreigners eventually gained control of Lower Egypt (the area from roughly Memphis north to the Mediterranean, including the massive Nile Delta) and ruled as pharaohs over the land for roughly a hundred years. The Israelites, like the Hyksos, were Semitic people. Both came from the Near East, and both were shepherds and farmers. It would not be surprising for a Hyksos pharaoh to make a Hebrew such as Joseph his prime minister and to allow the Israelites to settle in the land of the Delta with many other Semitic people.

Sometime after Joseph lived, Pharaoh Ahmose I of Upper Egypt (the area from roughly Memphis south), who ruled from 1550 to 1525 B.C., led an Egyptian army to defeat the Hyksos and drive them from Egypt. Ahmose united Upper and Lower Egypt once again and began what historians call the New Kingdom period of Egyptian history. Ahmose I may have been the "new king to whom Joseph meant nothing" who "came to power in Egypt." It would appear that the Israelites were not forced to leave Egypt with the Hyksos but allowed to remain. But the Egyptians had something else in mind for the Israelites.

> [Pharaoh] said to his people, "The Israelite people are now larger in number and stronger than we are. Come on, let's be smart and deal with them. Otherwise, they will only grow in number. And if war breaks out, they will join our enemies, fight against us, and then escape from the land." As a result, the Egyptians put foremen of forced work gangs over the Israelites to harass them with hard work.
>
> (Exodus 1:9-11)

Pharaoh feared that the Israelites would join Egypt's enemies, the Hyksos or other enemies from the east, and fight against Egypt in case of war, and he responded by enslaving the Israelites. *Fear* is a key word to remember in this part of Moses' story. It is behind the oppressive treatment of the Israelites at every turn.

Note what happens next:

> But the more they were oppressed, the more they grew and
> spread, so much so that the Egyptians started to look at the
> Israelites with disgust and dread. So the Egyptians enslaved
> the Israelites. They made their lives miserable with hard labor,
> making mortar and bricks, doing field work, and by forcing
> them to do all kinds of other cruel work.
>
> (Exodus 1:12-13)

Notice that Pharaoh was the most powerful ruler on earth, king
of both Upper and Lower Egypt, and yet he and his people were
anxious about a minority population of foreign sheepherders in their
midst. Their fear led them to despise the Israelites and to oppress
them.

And this is precisely where I'd like us to consider how the story
of Moses is more than just a story; it is Scripture that reveals truth
about us as human beings. What does the oppression of the Israelites
tell us about ourselves as a race or people?

Fear is a powerful emotion, and irrational fear can lead us to
do irrational and sometimes horrible things. It doesn't take long
to think of examples around the world in which fear of minority
populations has led nations to oppress, dehumanize, and at times kill
those viewed as strangers in their midst. The word we use for this fear
is *xenophobia*. Taken from the Greek, it means "fear of strangers."

I think of the ideal of America captured in Emma Lazarus's
famous lines, engraved on a bronze plaque inside the Statue of
Liberty:

> *Give me your tired, your poor,*
> *Your huddled masses yearning to breathe free,*
> *The wretched refuse of your teeming shore.*

Send these, the homeless, tempest-tost to me,
I lift my lamp beside the golden door!

Yet in our history there has always been a tension between living up to this lofty vision and our fear of the other. When the Irish came to America in large numbers in the mid-1800s because of a famine in their home country, fear gave birth to a new political group at first called the American Party and later the Know-Nothing Party. This group was certain the Irish were sent by the Pope to take over America, and they sought to ensure that Catholics would not hold office in America.

Later the Chinese came to America fleeing persecution in their own country. The United States happily received them, and at first even recruited them, as a source of cheap labor to build the railroads. But later, as the number of Chinese grew, they evoked fear and were spoken of as the "Yellow Peril." As a result of that fear, Congress passed the Chinese Exclusion Act of 1882 that prohibited all Chinese from entering America for the next sixty years.

By the 1920s, Americans were concerned with the Russians and anyone else from eastern Europe, including "undesirables" from Greece, Italy, Spain, and Czechoslovakia, as well as Jews. This new wave of fear led to the Immigration Act of 1924, which severely limited immigration of these groups while favoring "white" immigrants from Great Britain, France, and Germany. In this wave and others, two types of leaders were prone to use fear to motivate people into action: politicians and preachers.

However, our limits on immigration pale in comparison to the Nazi atrocities committed against Jews (as well as Gypsies, homosexuals, and a host of other groups). The Nazis were masters at instilling fear of the Jews and others into the hearts of the German people, a fear that led to unthinkable acts. Replaying the same siren song of fear in more recent times were the Khmer Rouge of Cambodia, the Hutu of Rwanda, various leaders in the Middle East, and too many more to name.

In Egypt, as fears grew about the increasing population of Hebrews, so too did the oppressive acts ordered by Pharaoh.

> The king of Egypt spoke to two Hebrew midwives named Shiphrah and Puah: "When you are helping the Hebrew women give birth and you see the baby being born, if it's a boy, kill him. But if it's a girl, you can let her live."
>
> (Exodus 1:15-16)

The Hebrews had not rebelled. They had done no harm to the Egyptians. Yet fear led Pharaoh to decree this dreadful plan to kill newborn baby boys.

Christians will remember a similar story, one that points back to this account, found at the beginning of Matthew's Gospel. King Herod the Great heard that a group of magi from Persia had read in the stars that a Hebrew child had been born who would become king of the Jews. In response, Herod, motivated by fear as Pharaoh had been, decreed the death of the Hebrew boys in Bethlehem.

If we're looking for ourselves in the story of Moses' birth, we've got to consider when and where we struggle with fear of the other and how our fears lead us to act in ways that are hardly humane.

Two Courageous Midwives

The writer of Exodus goes on to tell us something profound about the midwives who were commanded by Pharaoh to put the infant boys to death at childbirth: "Now the two midwives respected God so they didn't obey the Egyptian king's order. Instead, they let the baby boys live" (Exodus 1:17). These women feared God more than they feared Pharaoh, and they refused to go along with his plan. Can you imagine the courage of these two women? This is one of the first recorded acts of civil disobedience in history. Because of their disobedience they saved the lives of countless children, perhaps even that of Moses.

I want you to notice that while the pharaoh in this story is not named, the midwives' names are still known and celebrated 3,300 years later. Exodus tells us their names were Shiphrah and Puah.

How did these two midwives get away with disobeying Pharaoh? They lied to him! They told Pharaoh the Hebrew women were so strong that they had already given birth by the time the midwives had arrived. And God blessed them for their faith, courage, and willingness to do what was right, which in this case included being dishonest in order to protect the children. Here's what the text says: "So God treated the midwives well, and the people kept on multiplying and became very strong. And because the midwives respected God, God gave them households of their own" (Exodus 1:20-21).

This points to an interesting moral question: Is it ever okay to lie? We know we're not supposed to lie. And we know we're not supposed to kill. There are moments in life when we are faced with two competing ethical or moral claims—in this case, the ethical command not to lie and the ethical command not to kill. And we have to decide which of the two takes precedence. In the case of the midwives, they decided that saving lives took precedence over telling the truth, and it was the right call. It reminds me of the people who hid Jews in their homes during the Nazi Holocaust. When asked if they were harboring Jews, the people lied and their courageous acts were recognized as righteous. The decision of the midwives doesn't give us license to lie, but it does remind us that there are situations in which our reverence and respect and awe of God might lead us to violate one ethical imperative if it means keeping an even more important one.

Civil disobedience is another example. The Scriptures call us to obey authorities. But if the authorities ask us to do what is immoral—whether those authorities are military or political leaders, our bosses at work, or our teachers at school—the right thing to do is to disobey those authorities. A friend of mine recently quit a six-figure job when his company asked him to do something he felt in his heart was wrong. I was really proud of the courage he showed.

Roman Catholic Bishop Edward Daly died in 2016 after a remarkable ministry in Northern Ireland, where he was famous for challenging both the British government and the Irish Republican Army to end violence. Known as the "fearless peacebuilder," Daly stood up to both sides who felt violence was the only way to resolve the conflict, and he spoke out against the evils he saw around him. The bells of the cathedral in Derry rang out for an hour on news of his death.

In the story of Shiphrah and Puah, we find two remarkable women who remind us what courage looks like and who invite us to join them in resisting evil even if doing so comes at some personal cost. Here's the question I ask myself and would ask you: Are you willing to stand against the authorities if they call you to do something that is immoral or unjust?

A Determined Mother and
a Compassionate Princess

When the midwives refused to kill the boys as they were born, Pharaoh gave an order to *all* Egyptians: "Throw every baby boy born to the Hebrews into the Nile River, but you can let all the girls live" (1:22). Can you imagine? He called the entire Egyptian populace to tear children from their mother's arms and drown them in the Nile. And this is the context for the story of Moses' birth.

> Now a man from Levi's household married a Levite woman. The woman became pregnant and gave birth to a son. She saw that the baby was healthy and beautiful, so she hid him for three months. When she couldn't hide him any longer, she took a reed basket and sealed it up with black tar. She put the child in the basket and set the basket among the reeds at the riverbank. The baby's older sister stood watch nearby to see what would happen to him.
>
> (Exodus 2:1-4)

Moses' mother was Jochebed, a courageous woman who was not going to let her child be put to death. She refused to let her son die without attempting to save him. She hid him for three months, then took a basket made of reeds and she put her child in it and placed him among the reeds on the banks of the Nile. She did so at a location where Pharaoh's daughter was known to bathe, perhaps in hopes that the daughter would feel compassion for the child, disobey her father, and save the child.[5]

I want you to notice that this is the Bible's first story of adoption. Jochebed gave her child up for adoption in order to save his life. It was love that led her to give up the child; it was the only way she felt she could save him.

There are many people in the congregation I serve who have their own adoption stories, either having given up a child for adoption, having adopted, or themselves having been given up for adoption. One woman shared with me her story of giving up her child:

> I gave up my firstborn for adoption thirty-seven
> years ago. I was twenty-three, alone and scared.
> While so very painful, mine is a beautiful story. I can
> say without hesitancy that even through the darkest
> days of my experience, being totally isolated from
> family and friends, I felt the hand of God cover me
> throughout my whole journey. I wanted to keep
> her, but I felt that she should not have to do "hard"
> because of me. She deserved better. I prayed daily
> that God would protect my daughter.... Sometimes,
> years later, I would wake up in the middle of the
> night and she would be on my heart.... Four years
> ago she found me. Her family is beautiful, and
> they raised her to be a strong woman of faith. She
> thanked me for giving her life. She has a beautiful
> family of her own. I am still sorry for any hurt that
> I caused by that decision years ago, but I am forever
> grateful to God for watching over her, and me.

Some of you, like Moses, were adopted. Some, like Moses' mother Jochebed, gave your children up for adoption, not because you didn't care but because you cared deeply for your child and sought to save them and give them a future with hope.

The Nile River at Luxor

And that leads us to consider Pharaoh's daughter. We don't know anything about her except that she saw the Hebrew child and, despite knowing what her father had decreed regarding Israelite boys, felt compassion and pity for the child and was moved to adopt him. How easy it would have been for her to have left the child there in the basket on the banks of the Nile, perhaps fearing her father or believing that surely *someone else* would save him. But instead her compassion led her to lift the child from the water, risk her father's wrath, and take him home, adopting him as her own child.

Of the four courageous women who saved the baby Moses, Pharaoh's daughter was the least likely.[6] She was the daughter of a despot who was oppressing and killing Israelites. She worshiped the Egyptian gods and goddesses. Yet God used her, as Moses' adoptive parent, in one of the most important roles played by any mother in human history.

I wonder if God may be calling some of you reading these words to the ministry of adoption or offering foster care for a child in need of parents. This may be part of God's word to you from this story.

The Providence of God

The story of Moses' birth and how he was spared from death in Exodus helps us see how God typically works in our world. We often pray for God's miraculous intervention in the world. In the case of Moses, his mother undoubtedly prayed again and again for God to spare her son. But notice, God didn't send angels from heaven to spare him. God didn't miraculously step in to destroy Pharaoh or change his heart.

No, two midwives feared God and courageously practiced civil disobedience when they saved many Hebrew children, likely including Moses. A heroic mother saved Moses when she hatched a plan for Pharaoh's daughter to adopt him. A princess who listened to her heart rather than to her father's decrees took this child in and made him her own son.

Owing to the actions of these four heroic women, Moses survived and was raised in the pharaoh's household, where he would receive the finest education money could buy, and which ultimately would prepare him for God's mission—a mission to challenge a future pharaoh, to lead the children of Israel out of bondage, and to form a new nation.

There's one last thing I want you to notice as you read Exodus 2: 1-10, the story of Moses' birth, his deliverance from Pharaoh's deadly decree, and his adoption into Pharaoh's house: God is hardly mentioned in these verses, and yet it's clear that God was active through these various women. I mention this because it illustrates the way God usually works in our world—through people. When we listen to our hearts, do what we know is right, and pay attention to the nudges and promptings and whispers of the Spirit, we find ourselves being used by God to accomplish his purposes. God uses ordinary people, in seemingly ordinary ways, to do extraordinary things.

Notice too that God works through disappointing and difficult circumstances. Moses' mother had to give up her baby to save him, but God was there working through this heartbreaking situation. Moses as a child was likely teased for being the one drawn out of the water, for having no father, for being adopted, but God was at work then as well, likely using such experiences to foster compassion in Moses' heart. God often works most profoundly in the disappointment and heartache of our lives.

To summarize, there's much we can learn from the story of Moses' early life: Don't give in to fear of the other, as Pharaoh did. When those in authority call you to do what you know is wrong, resist them, as Shiphrah and Puah did. When you face heartbreaking circumstances, trust that God is still at work, as Moses' mother Jochebed did. And when you see those in need, let your heart be moved to compassion, as the Egyptian princess did. If you do these things, you may find yourself playing a pivotal role in God's saving story.

Walking Where Moses Walked: A Visit to Luxor

In each chapter I'll share with you a few of the things you would see if you were walking in the footsteps of Moses. I'm including

Hot air balloons at sunrise over the Valley of the Kings

photos of some of these locations, and in the video designed to accompany this book I will take you to these locations.

As with Cairo, we arrived in Luxor just after sunset. We checked into our hotel on the eastern bank of the Nile River. Across the Nile we could see the desert mountains and the plateau we knew to be the Valley of the Kings. I woke early the next morning and watched the sun rising upon the mountains with beautiful hues of pink and orange. Hot air balloons were lifting off, taking visiting tourists for a flight over the ancient necropolis. We were in Luxor two nights, and both mornings I couldn't resist getting up early to watch the sunrise. It was truly magnificent.

We began our first day in Luxor visiting Pharaoh Hatshepsut's mortuary temple, beautifully preserved and restored just south of the Valley of the Kings. Hatshepsut, a woman, ruled as the pharaoh for approximately twenty years, from 1478 to 1458 B.C. If an early date is assumed for the Exodus, then she would have been the pharaoh ruling just prior to those events.

We then toured the Valley of the Kings. Beginning in the 1500s B.C., Egypt's kings began to build elaborate underground burial chambers. Each pharaoh would commission a tomb shortly after ascending the throne. The tombs, like the earlier pyramids, would have walls with careful instructions for the journey to the afterlife, the judgment, and the king's deification. Rooms in the burial chambers would be filled with items deemed necessary for a successful afterlife, including food, drink, furniture, and chariots.

Most of the sixty-three tombs and hundreds of chambers in the tombs had been sacked by grave robbers over the millennia, but in 1922, archaeologist Howard Carter and his team discovered a tomb that was largely intact: the tomb of King Tutankhamun, known to us as King Tut. This boy king ruled just nine years, from 1332 to 1323 B.C. If a late date is assumed for the Exodus, then Tutankhamun was the pharaoh when Moses was in his late teens and into his twenties. King Tutankhamun was nine years old when he began to rule and only eighteen when he died. Many of the treasures that were found in the tomb are now in the Egyptian Museum in Cairo. The dry conditions in the Valley of the Kings preserved most of the items in his grave amazingly well. You can see his chariots, several beds, thrones, jewelry, and so much more. The items from Tut's tomb allow us to see actual objects from the time of Moses' story.

While touring the Valley of the Kings, we visited three tombs, each with multiple burial chambers. It was astounding to see how well preserved the paintings and hieroglyphics on the walls were. The colors were still vibrant more than 3,300 years after the artisans first created those images on the walls.

Massive columns at the Karnak Temple

From the Valley of the Kings, we went to the Karnak Temple. This complex, the second largest temple complex in the world, was built over a period of nearly two thousand years, starting sometime around 1950 B.C. by Pharaoh Senusret I, with the final buildings added just prior to the time of Christ. In all, over thirty pharaohs constructed buildings or monuments at the complex. Among the amazing features at Karnak is the "hypostyle hall," a massive room with 134 giant columns, most of which are thirty feet tall. If a late date is assumed for Moses, this hall was built during his lifetime by Seti I and Ramesses II. The exterior walls of the temples of Karnak and Luxor are carved with battle scenes in which various pharaohs were victorious over their enemies.

The entire Karnak complex is simply awe-inspiring. The complex and other temples in Luxor were places where, as a young man, Moses would have seen sacred architecture and the offering of sacrifices to

Altar at the Karnak Temple

the gods. These sights, in turn, would have shaped his own thinking as he later gave instructions for building the Tent of Meeting or Tabernacle—the worship space erected by the Israelites during the Exodus—along with its furnishings and the offerings that were made there.

On the columns and interior walls at Karnak are scenes of the pharaohs offering sacrifices to the gods, sacrifices at times very similar to the sacrifices required in the Torah. Just as the Tent of Meeting had a Holy Place and a Most Holy Place (Holy of Holies), so too did the temples of Karnak and Luxor. The altars in Karnak and at other locations are similar in size and shape to the altar in the Tent of Meeting.

Later, we took a tour of the Luxor Temple by night, where giant statues of Pharaoh Ramesses II seated on his throne greeted us. Again, assuming a later date for the Exodus, Ramesses II was likely

Luxor Temple by night

the pharaoh Moses confronted to demand the release of the Israelite slaves. Some scholars believe that this temple was dedicated to the pharaohs themselves and that their coronations may have taken place here. It is also believed that the temple was dedicated in some way to the concept of the pharaohs' divinity, showing that while the pharaohs were mortal, they also were imbued with a divine force that gave them the authority to rule. The pharaoh was thought to become entirely divine after death, but while living the pharaoh was seen as the intermediary, a kind of high priest, interceding on behalf of the people.

Seeing these temples gave me a deep appreciation for just how epic a battle Moses faced when he confronted Pharaoh and demanded the release of the Israelite slaves. We'll consider this battle in a subsequent chapter.

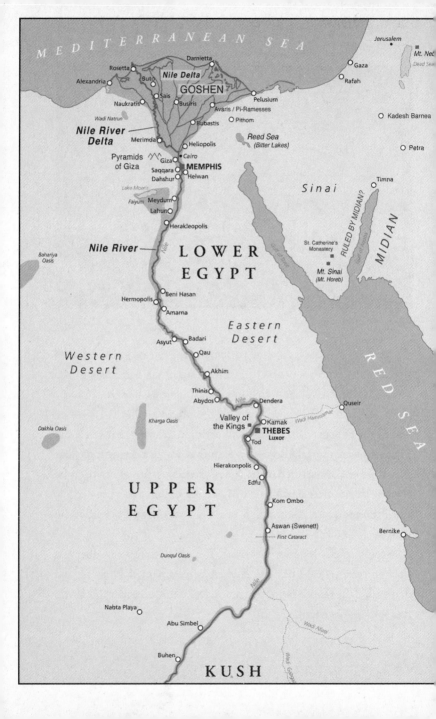

2.

TWO MOMENTS THAT DEFINED THE MAN

In the last chapter we left Moses as an infant, given up for adoption by his mother, Jochebed, in order to save his life. Pharaoh's daughter took him in, and he became part of the large royal family likely living in Thebes. The story in Exodus tells us nothing more about his childhood or adolescence, though Acts 7:22 expresses the rabbinic tradition that "Moses learned everything Egyptian wisdom had to offer, and he was a man of powerful words and deeds."

Following his birth and adoption by Pharaoh's daughter, the Exodus account immediately moves to a pivotal moment in Moses' life, when he was a young man. (Acts 7:23 tells us this occurred when

Moses was forty, reflecting a rabbinic tradition that marked the key events in Moses' life happening at birth, age forty, age eighty, and age 120.) Like the other young nobles, Moses grew up in the lap of luxury. He and the hundreds of other royal family members wanted for nothing. They would have traveled up and down the Nile as part of their education and oversight of Egypt, from modern-day Aswan in the south, to the pyramids at Giza and the city of Memphis, and on to the Mediterranean Sea.

It seems clear that, as he was growing up, Moses knew he was adopted and realized that his own people were the Hebrews.[1] The Hebrews, or Israelites, had originally settled in the Nile River Delta, and based on the Exodus story it appears that most continued to live in the Delta, the historic "Land of Goshen." Thus, the pivotal moment described in Exodus probably occurred there.

Exodus 2:11 tells us, "One day after Moses had become an adult, he went out among his people and he saw their forced labor." When I read this passage I'm reminded of several people I know who were adopted and who at some point wanted to meet their family of origin. I'm also reminded of the Buddha, who lived seven hundred years after Moses. He was raised in a royal palace and shielded from suffering, but as a young man he left the palace to meet the common people and was moved by their suffering. In so many ways, the much earlier story of Moses captures a similar theme.

Moses likely witnessed the suffering of the Israelites in the Delta, perhaps in the area around the ancient city of Avaris, the capital of the Lower Kingdom of Egypt during the time of the patriarch Joseph. So we traveled to this region on our journey in the footsteps of Moses. Few Christian visitors travel to this region anymore, as the archaeological sites related to Moses and the Exodus are difficult to reach and the U.S. State Department requires an armed guard and military escort to reach them.

I'll tell you more about the Nile Delta in chapter 3. For now I simply want to recount what happened at this pivotal moment in Moses' life. When Moses saw an Egyptian taskmaster beating a Hebrew slave, compassion for the slave and indignation toward the Egyptian led Moses to kill the taskmaster. He buried him in the sand. Unbeknownst to Moses, however, someone had seen him kill the Egyptian. When Pharaoh learned that Moses had killed an Egyptian taskmaster, Moses was immediately perceived to be a traitor and a threat. Consequently, Moses fled Egypt. Exodus 2:15 tells us, "Moses ran away from Pharaoh and settled down in the land of Midian."

Moses in the Land of Midian

Moses settled in Midian, but where was Midian? The answer is not clear. Today we recognize that Midian was located in western Saudi Arabia, but some suggest that the Midian referred to in Scripture wasn't so much a particular place but a confederation of tribes in the region and that some of the Midianites lived in parts of the Sinai Peninsula.

Did Moses make his way to western Saudi Arabia and settle there? Or did he settle in the Sinai, among a clan or clans of the Midianites? We can't know for certain, but the traditional location for the next chapter in Moses' life is in south central Sinai, in and around St. Catherine's Monastery.[2] For at least 1,700 to 1,800 years, perhaps much longer, Christians and Jews, and later, Muslims, have visited this region in the belief that it was the home of Moses and the site of Mount Sinai.

St. Catherine's Monastery as seen from above, with mountains in the background

With that in mind, we drove from the eastern Nile River Delta to Mount Sinai, a distance of about 215 miles. We passed under the Suez Canal using the Ahmed Hamdi Tunnel while large tankers passed overhead. The tunnel is ten miles north of the Red Sea. Exiting the tunnel, we headed south on the El Tor Road, with the Red Sea to our right and the Sinai desert to our left. This was the same journey that Exodus tells us Moses made three times during his lifetime (fleeing from Pharaoh, returning to confront Pharaoh, and leading the Israelites out of Egypt).

The farther south one travels in the Sinai, the more mountainous the terrain becomes and the more ruggedly beautiful. From time to time an oasis, identified by its grove of palm trees, punctuates the land. Wells provide water for small villages and for the Bedouin shepherds who can be seen tending their flocks along the way.

Eventually, we turned east on St. Catherine's Highway, traveling into the heart of the Sinai Peninsula. It's here that the real beauty begins. The highway winds its way through mountains formed by volcanic activity eons ago. Mountain peaks rise over seven thousand feet, and the vistas, particularly at sunset, are breathtaking. Tradition has it that somewhere in this vast land, likely a month after fleeing Egypt, Moses came upon a well where the nomadic shepherds watered their sheep. Here's what Scripture tells us happened next:

> One day Moses was sitting by a well. Now there was a
> Midianite priest who had seven daughters. The daughters
> came to draw water and fill the troughs so that their father's
> flock could drink. But some shepherds came along and rudely
> chased them away. Moses got up, rescued the women, and
> gave their flock water to drink.
>
> (Exodus 2:15-17)

As we drove through that part of the Sinai, it wasn't hard to picture this scene. We passed shepherd girls, young women who appeared to be in their teens, walking with their sheep and goats along the road, dressed much as I imagine shepherd girls dressed 3,300 years ago. We saw wells at various oases, places where travelers today, much as Moses did millennia ago, met locals and made arrangements for lodging and food.[3]

As Moses approached the well, he saw the young women being harassed and felt the same sense of compassion and righteous indignation he had felt seeing the Hebrew slave beaten. He came to their aid, much as he had done in fighting for the slave a month or so earlier.

In these two scenes from Moses' life—his observation of the beating of the Israelite slave, and the moment he witnessed the

Shepherd girl tending her flock in the Sinai

harassment of the shepherd girls—we learn some important things about Moses. He was angered by injustice, and he was compelled to rectify it. Moses had compassion for those who were picked on, harassed, or oppressed, and he had the courage to act in protecting those who were being mistreated.

Often those who have the greatest compassion for others and the keenest sense of injustice are those who themselves have experienced injustice, bullying, or harassment, and that brings us to the matter of Moses' name. Exodus 2:10 says that when Moses was drawn out of the river by Pharaoh's daughter, "She named him Moses, 'because,' she said, 'I pulled him out of the water.'" The footnote in your Bible may tell you that the name Moses sounds like the Hebrew word *mashah*, which means "to pull out."

Now, it's possible that Pharaoh's daughter did indeed choose a Hebrew word as the name for her adopted son, and if she did, then

Moses' name would have been a constant reminder that he was adopted and pulled out of the Nile River. But more likely, she chose an Egyptian name for her son. Moses is likely a form of an Egyptian word, transliterated into English as *mose*, which in its various forms meant "born of," or "son of." Typically such a name included a prefix, and that prefix was often the name of an Egyptian god. For example, among the pharaohs we have Thutmose, son of the god Thoth. There is Ramesses or Ramessu (*messes* or *messu* being another form of *mose*), son of the god Ra. There is Ahmose I, born of the god Iah. But in the case of Moses, a child who was found in the Nile and adopted by Pharaoh's daughter, choosing the name Moses might have been a way of marking him as one whose father was unknown. He was simply *mose* without a prefix: a son without a father. One can imagine that as Moses was growing up, his name might have been the source of pain, knowing he was either the boy drawn out of the water or a young man who was "son of no one." One wonders how much teasing, maybe even bullying, Moses endured for this name as he was growing up.

For Moses and for all of us, the painful parts of our past can make us either bitter and resentful, or stronger and more compassionate. I think of Justin Timberlake, who grew up in Tennessee and because he wasn't into sports but instead acting, was teased and made to feel he was an outcast. Comedian Chris Rock says that he was bullied beginning in second grade as the only African American in his school in New York. He was picked on, beat up, and spit at, but he maintains that it was "the defining experience of my life…it made me who I am." Lady Gaga and Taylor Swift were both teased and bullied as kids, and it led both to a deep sense of compassion for those who are bullied.[4]

So Moses, perhaps motivated by his own struggles as a boy, defended the young women at the well, drove away the shepherds who harassed them, and then watered their sheep for them.

Moses the Shepherd

As recounted in Exodus 2:19-22, the young women left Moses and returned home to their father with the flock, probably earlier than expected because Moses had helped them. They told their father how "an Egyptian man rescued us from a bunch of shepherds. Afterward, he even helped us draw water to let the flock drink."

Their father, here called Reuel,[5] asked, "So where is he? Why did you leave this man? Invite him to eat a meal with us." Moses accepted the invitation, and soon Reuel "gave his daughter Zipporah to Moses as his wife." Zipporah bore a child, and Moses settled in the region with his family, tending his father-in-law's sheep.

Within just a month or so, Moses had gone from being a prince in Egypt, to a fugitive from the law, and finally a married nomadic shepherd among the Midianites. Shepherds were considered by the Egyptians to be among the lowest groups in society, as Genesis 46:34 notes: "Egyptians think all shepherds are beneath their dignity." Moses stayed in this region, tending the flocks, for the next forty years.

As I walked around the rocky and barren wilderness near Mount Sinai, I thought about Moses' life during those forty years. Standing among the rugged, treeless mountains, I wondered: How many times did Moses reflect on the life of luxury he had once lived? How often did he think about the Israelite slaves and their oppression back in Egypt? Did he lose faith while driving his sheep in the wilderness, given that his life had turned out so differently than he had hoped or dreamed of as a young man? What I want you to notice is just how far Moses had fallen from his place as a nobleman in Egypt.

Moses' forty years in the wilderness is in some ways a metaphor for events in our own lives—periods when things are not going well, when we experience downward mobility, or when we feel like abject failures. Some reading this book know what it is to have once been on top—successful, wealthy, living the dream—only to lose it all and end up struggling with feelings of being "washed up." They've lived in the wilderness. I've seen this happen many times with people in the congregation I serve, particularly after the Great Recession. I've watched people who had made millions weeping when they lost it all and could not find employment. Two men I knew felt so defeated that they took their own lives.

It may surprise you to know that some of the most important Old Testament figures spent years in their own wilderness—seasons in which life was very, very hard. Abraham knew many trials, not least of which were the years when he and his wife Sarah struggled with infertility. David had to live in caves and among the Philistines for years when King Saul sought to kill him. Later, Israel's enemies routinely attacked him. David is said to have written many of his most powerful psalms during such times. Elijah the prophet, facing hardship as Jezebel tried to kill him, actually fled to the same wilderness where Moses had settled and there waited to hear from God.

While it wasn't God who forced Moses to the wilderness as a fugitive, God did use Moses' season in the wilderness to prepare him to lead the children of Israel once they left Egypt As for our own wilderness experiences, they might be the result of a bad economy, illness or loss, harmful decisions made by others, or decisions we've made ourselves; they are seldom God's will or work. Nevertheless,

The wilderness of Sinai

God uses our seasons in the wilderness, if we allow him to, in order to prepare and shape our hearts, minds, and character for his good purposes.

During the first forty years of Moses' life, living in Thebes, he learned the Egyptian language, culture, philosophy, and religion; he learned economics, construction, leadership, and doubtless many other important skills. But during the next forty years of his life, during his time in the wilderness, he learned things that may have been even more important: humility, perseverance, self-discipline, faith, character, and how to listen for the voice of God. All these qualities would enable him to forge the children of Israel into a new nation and then help them survive in the wilderness.

God is not finished with us because we're in the wilderness; in fact, God is often most profoundly at work in us during the wilderness seasons of our lives. In the case of Moses, those forty years were preparing him for the most important part of his story.

The Burning Bush

Forty years passed in Moses' life. He had long since traded his home in the royal palace for a nomad's tent in the rugged Sinai, and he had two sons with his wife Zipporah.[6] Moses spent most of each year living in tents and driving his flocks of sheep, goats, and possibly even camels to find what little vegetation grew in the desert. Parts of the Sinai receive as little as an inch and a quarter of rainfall annually. Other places along the Mediterranean Sea receive an average of six inches, and the area around St. Catherine's Monastery receives about two and a half inches. By comparison, Kansas City, where I live, gets about forty inches of rain each year. My point is that the nomadic herders in the Sinai learned the skill of moving their flocks to find vegetation in a very dry region, a skill that would serve Moses well when leading God's flock, the Israelites, through the Sinai.

Exodus tells us virtually nothing about this forty-year period of Moses' life; in fact, the entire time from age forty when Moses killed the Egyptian, to age eighty when Moses met God at a burning bush, comprises only twelve verses. Exodus 2:23-25 marks the author's transition from Moses settling in Midian to God's call for him to return to Egypt:

> A long time passed, and the Egyptian king died. The Israelites were still groaning because of their hard work. They cried out, and their cry to be rescued from the hard work rose up to God. God heard their cry of grief, and God remembered his covenant with Abraham, Isaac, and Jacob. God looked at the Israelites, and God understood.

I love this passage. It tells us that God "heard" the cries of the Israelites; God "remembered" his covenant with Abraham, Isaac, and

Jacob; God "looked" at the Israelites; and God "understood." God then acted to get Moses' attention, calling him to be God's leader who would deliver the Israelites from bondage. Exodus 3 begins with these words:

> Moses was taking care of the flock for his father-in-law Jethro, Midian's priest. He led his flock out to the edge of the desert, and he came to God's mountain called Horeb.
>
> (Exodus 3:1)

It is interesting that Moses' father-in-law, previously referred to as Reuel, here is called "Jethro, Midian's priest." The Midianites were descendants of Abraham through Abraham's second wife, Keturah (Genesis 25:2). They were cousins of the Israelites. There were multiple tribes of Midianites, and some Midianite city-states had kings over them (at least five are mentioned in Numbers). Like most of the people in the ancient Near East, they seem to have worshiped a variety of gods, including Yahweh. It seems likely that during the forty years when Moses took care of his flock, Jethro, as "Midian's priest," taught Moses about the gods of the Midianites including Yahweh, whom Moses was about to meet in a dramatic fashion.[7]

But on this particular day, when Moses was tending Jethro's flock near Mount Horeb, he saw something most unusual—a bush that was burning but not being consumed—and a voice called out his name.

> The LORD's messenger appeared to him in a flame of fire in the middle of a bush. Moses saw that the bush was in flames, but it didn't burn up. Then Moses said to himself, Let me check out this amazing sight and find out why the bush isn't burning up.

> When the LORD saw that he was coming to look, God called
> to him out of the bush, "Moses, Moses!" Moses said, "I'm
> here." Then the LORD said, "Don't come any closer! Take off
> your sandals, because you are standing on holy ground."
>
> (Exodus 3:2-5)

In the Old Testament, the "LORD's messenger" appears at some points to be a separate being (the word *messenger* is also translated as *angel*) while at other points this seems to be a way of referring to God's direct appearance to an individual.

God's appearance at Mount Horeb was in the form of flames in a bush. God often appeared in Scripture in the midst of flames. In Genesis 15:17 God appeared to Abraham as a "fiery flame." Beginning in Exodus 13, God would lead the Israelites as a "pillar of fire" (NRSV). Later, when God appeared to the Israelites in Exodus 24:17, "The LORD's glorious presence looked like a blazing fire on top of the mountain." In Daniel 7:9, God sat on a throne ablaze with flames. In Acts 2, when the Holy Spirit descends upon the disciples, the Spirit appeared as flames of fire. And Hebrews 12:28-29 (NIV) tells Christians to "worship God acceptably with reverence and awe, for our 'God is a consuming fire.'"

God called Moses by name from the bush, then warned him not to come any closer and commanded, "Take off your sandals, because you are standing on holy ground." Sandals carried soil, and it was a sign of respect to remove them when entering a home or place of worship. In addition, people always took off their sandals in the presence of Pharaoh; failing to do so showed disrespect. Muslims today continue this tradition in their mosques. I've been in mosques in various parts of the world, and the practice is the same: shoes are left on the ground or in bins just outside the entrance.[8]

This command from God that Moses remove his shoes, despite the fact that he was standing outside in the wilderness, was a sign that any place where God appears is holy and that the appropriate response to an encounter with God is reverence and respect. In various cultures the donning of hats, or the removing of them, is an expression of respect when in worship or prayer. In Jerusalem, Jews back away from the Western Wall where thousands go daily to pray, unwilling to turn their backs on this sacred place that represents God's house. Atop the Temple Mount, which Muslims call the Haram al-Sharif, Muslims wash their feet and hands before entering either the Al-Aqsa Mosque or the Dome of the Rock, again as a sign of reverence and respect.

Many Christians have lost this sense of reverence, respect, and awe when gathering for worship. In our focus on friendship and intimacy with God, and our emphasis on the grace and acceptance of God, we sometimes forget that "our God is a consuming fire" and that he demanded of Moses the ancient Near Eastern sign of respect, the removal of one's sandals. I wonder, what signs of respect does God demand of us today?

Consider what God says next to Moses:

> He continued, "I am the God of your father, Abraham's God, Isaac's God, and Jacob's God." Moses hid his face because he was afraid to look at God. Then the LORD said, "I've clearly seen my people oppressed in Egypt. I've heard their cry of injustice because of their slave masters. I know about their pain. I've come down to rescue them from the Egyptians.... So get going. I'm sending you to Pharaoh to bring my people, the Israelites, out of Egypt."
>
> (Exodus 3:6-8, 10)

I love this text. Once more God reveals something about himself to Moses, similar to what we read at the end of Exodus 2: God has "seen" the oppression of slaves in Egypt; God has "heard" their cries of injustice; and God "knows" their pain. I believe the same is true wherever God's people are oppressed or hurting today. God continues to be concerned for those who are marginalized. He is concerned about the people who are teased, picked on, abused, and hurt. He sees, he hears, and he knows their pain.

Notice how, having seen, heard, and known the pain of the Israelites, God responded. He did not send a legion of angels to liberate the Israelite slaves from Egypt. No, God showed up in a burning bush to an eighty-year-old shepherd! And not just any eighty-year-old shepherd. He found a shepherd who was fluent in the Egyptian language, who had been an insider when it came to Egyptian power and rule, and who knew philosophy, religion, law, governance, and leadership. He called an eighty-year-old shepherd who once had felt such indignation at the oppression of the Israelites that he killed a man to stop it. God didn't send an angel; he sent a person. God said to Moses, "Get going! I'm sending you!" We're not meant to miss this: God sometimes chooses, calls, and uses the most unlikely of people to do his work in the world.

This is such an important point that I want to make sure we get it. God's usual way of working in the world to alleviate suffering, injustice, and pain is not to intervene miraculously, suspending the laws of nature, violating the principle of human freedom, or sending angels to make things right. No, God works through people. God sees, hears, and knows the suffering of others. God expects his people to do the same. And God's response is to call us to step up as instruments of his aid. While I was writing this chapter, people were recovering from massive flooding in the United States and the Caribbean. Does God care? Absolutely. And God's response is to say to his people who are paying attention, "Get going! I'm sending you!"

Occasionally, we may have the kind of burning bush experience Moses had when we hear the audible voice of God or when events clearly reflect God's call on our lives. But in my experience, God's call most often comes in a whisper or through a feeling, nudge, or compulsion that I can't shake. I hear the voice of God most often when I'm reading, praying, or discussing the faith with others or when I'm worshiping, singing, or listening to the Scriptures read aloud or preached. Sometimes I hear God's call when I'm watching the news and seeing stories of pain and suffering. In the church I serve, most of the major initiatives we have taken to address poverty or injustice in the Kansas City metropolitan area came to us as we listened to the news or heard others describing places where people needed love, encouragement, help, and support.

St. Catherine's Monastery in the Sinai

As far back as the time of Elijah, in the ninth century before Christ, people made their way to Mount Sinai, or Mount Horeb as it is also called, in the hope of encountering God as Moses had done. (Elijah's journey to Mount Horeb is described in 1 Kings 19.) In the late second or early third century A.D., Christians came to the southern Sinai and lived as hermits or in small communities, seeking God among the stark, rugged mountains where they believed Moses had met God over a millennium earlier. It is believed that in the A.D. 300s, Helen, mother of Constantine, the emperor who is often

St. Catherine's Monastery

credited with converting the Roman Empire to Christianity, built a chapel at the base of one of these mountains.. Two hundred years after that, Emperor Justinian constructed the church, walls, and some of the other buildings that today we know as St. Catherine's Monastery, the focal point of which was the Church of the Transfiguration. The oldest continuously used Christian monastery in the world, St. Catherine's is a UNESCO world heritage site and continues to be the home of twenty to thirty monks.

The chapel Helen built, known as the Chapel of the Burning Bush, was incorporated into the Church of the Transfiguration. A well within the monastery complex identifies the supposed place where Moses met Zipporah. A large bush of the variety *Rubus sanctus* is said to have been growing there when the first monks arrived on this site and was believed to be the bush from which God spoke to Moses. The original location of the bush is marked by a silver star in the floor of the Chapel of the Burning Bush. (The bush was moved

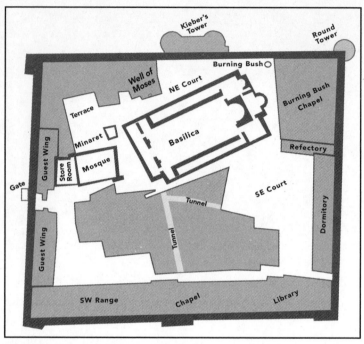

Map of St. Catherine's Monastery complex

a few yards away to its present location presumably when the chapel was built.) The fourth-century Christian pilgrim Egeria wrote about a bush on this site that was considered to be the burning bush where God met Moses.

We arrived at St. Catherine's late in the afternoon. My heart beat faster as we approached the ancient walls of the monastery. For years I had studied pictures of the place and dreamed of visiting it myself. I was struck by how much larger the mountains surrounding the monastery appeared to be when I was standing in front of them, compared with the photos I had seen. Though the claim seems incredible to me that the bush at St. Catherine's was *the* bush of Moses

This bush in the monastery complex, called the Burning Bush, is a visible reminder of Moses' encounter with God.

or that the well was *the* well where Moses met Zipporah, the fact that thousands of pilgrims have come to the site to recall the story has made it holy ground, whether or not it was the exact location of Moses' call.

The monastery is also home to a collection of beautiful and very old icons, which we were able to see, along with a library of priceless ancient manuscripts kept by the monks. One of the oldest and most important complete New Testament manuscripts was found in the library of St. Catherine's. Known as Codex Sinaiticus, it dates back to the fourth century and includes the entire New Testament (with the addition of two books that were often debated by the early church: the Epistle of Barnabas and parts of the Shepherd of Hermas), as well as much of the Old Testament and the Apocrypha.[9]

Moses, a Reluctant Prophet

Let's return to Moses as he stood before the burning bush. He was eighty years old. He hadn't been to Egypt in forty years. During that period, he had likely buried within himself the concern he had once felt for his own people. He had tried to block from his mind the thoughts of what he'd seen in the land of Goshen, where the Israelites were being oppressed by the Egyptians.

God knew that deep down inside, Moses still remembered and was still concerned for the people to whom he'd been born. But now, standing before the bush and hearing God tell him, "Get going. I'm sending you," Moses responded as most of us would—he began making excuses.

> Moses said to God, "Who am I to go to Pharaoh and to bring the Israelites out of Egypt?"
>
> God said, "I'll be with you."

(Exodus 3:11-12)

God frequently repeated this response throughout the Bible when God's people were frightened about the journey ahead: "Don't be afraid. I'll be with you." In fact, it's said that over a hundred times in Scripture God called his people not to be afraid, and the reason was nearly always the same: "I am with you."

Moses didn't stop at that first excuse. Next he said to God,

> "If I now come to the Israelites and say to them, 'The God of your ancestors has sent me to you,' they are going to ask me, 'What's this God's name?' What am I supposed to say to them?"

(Exodus 3:13)

The passage points to the fact that the Israelites, like the Egyptians and the Midianites, had by this time likely embraced the idea that there were many deities. Moses wanted to know which of these many deities had appeared before him. The response:

> God said to Moses, "I Am Who I Am. So say to the Israelites, 'I Am has sent me to you.'" God continued, "Say to the Israelites, 'The LORD, the God of your ancestors, Abraham's

God, Isaac's God, and Jacob's God, has sent me to you.'
This is my name forever; this is how all generations will
remember me."

(Exodus 3:14-15)

Let's pause here to ponder the meaning of this odd name. In Hebrew the divine name YHWH is closely related to the word translated "I Am" in the statement God made to Moses: "I Am Who I Am." Scholars are not entirely sure how to pronounce this name or what it means, and faithful Jews stopped pronouncing it long ago out of reverence and respect for God's name. The Hebrew alphabet has only consonants, no vowels, so we have to guess which vowel sounds to provide when pronouncing the name. We believe the correct pronunciation is *Yahweh*.[10]

We're not completely sure how to translate this statement or what God intended by it, but many see it as meaning something like "I am being itself" or "I am existence itself," or perhaps better, "I am the source of all things." Everything that is exists because God is; or, as the Apostle Paul noted in his words before the philosophers of first-century Athens, quoting the ancient Greek poet Epimenides, "In him we live and move and have our being."

In instructing Moses to tell the Israelites, "I Am has sent me to you," God was offering a profound truth that it seems unlikely the Israelites would have fully comprehended; in fact, I don't believe we fully comprehend it: the God who has seen their suffering and intends to act on their behalf is none other than the Source, the Creative Power, and the Sustainer of everything that exists.

God is everywhere, and God's power and will make possible everything that is; but God is never simply to be equated with everything that exists, anymore than the sculptor should be equated with the sculpture. The sculpture would not exist were it not for the sculptor, but the sculptor is greater than, and distinct from, the sculptor's creation. In essence, God was inviting Moses to tell the Israelites, "The one who made heaven and earth and all that is in them, the one from whom you derive your existence—that one cares about you, has seen your suffering, hears your prayers, and intends to deliver you."

Having learned the name of the God who was addressing him, Moses offered another objection.

> Then Moses replied, "But what if they don't believe me or pay attention to me? They might say to me, 'The LORD didn't appear to you!'"
>
> (Exodus 4:1)

In response, God instructed Moses to throw down his shepherd's rod, and God turned it into a snake. God told Moses to pick up the snake, and it turned back into a rod. Next God asked Moses to put his hand inside his coat. When Moses took his hand back out, he saw it was afflicted with a terrible skin disease. Then, when God asked Moses to put his hand back inside his coat and take it out again, his hand had been healed. These miracles were offered as proofs that Moses could show the Israelites so they would believe him.

Even seeing the miracles, Moses made more excuses.

> But Moses said to the LORD, "My Lord, I've never been able to speak well, not yesterday, not the day before, and certainly not now since you've been talking to your servant. I have a slow mouth and a thick tongue."
>
> (Exodus 4:10)

Did Moses actually stutter, or did he simply struggle as many do with public speaking? We can't know, but clearly God wasn't interested in hearing it.

> Then the LORD said to him, "Who gives people the ability to speak? Who's responsible for making them unable to speak or hard of hearing, sighted or blind? Isn't it I, the LORD? Now go! I'll help you speak, and I'll teach you what you should say."
>
> (Exodus 4:11-12)

Finally, having run out of excuses, Moses simply blurted out, "Please, my Lord, just send someone else" (4:13). Remember, these stories were told and retold over generations, and it's easy to imagine the smiles on listeners' faces as they heard this scene unfold, particularly given Moses' final attempt to weasel out of God's call. I love the humanity of Moses that we see in this exchange. Once more the man who would be known as the Great Liberator and the Lawgiver is seen to be a very reluctant servant of God.

At times, all of us feel like making excuses for failing to do what we fear deep in our hearts that God is calling us to do. I suspect there has been a moment in your life when you've reacted in this way. Now imagine if God had responded to Moses' objections by saying, "No problem Moses, I'll find someone else. You just keep tending your father-in-law's sheep here in the Sinai." Moses would have missed out on the most important moment of his life, the epic event for which his entire story up to that point had been preparing him. He would have missed being used by God to deliver an entire nation of people from slavery to freedom. He would have missed shaping and forming these people to be God's own people. He would have missed seeing the Promised Land. And you would not be reading a book about him 3,300 years later.

Every one of us is called, repeatedly, to be God's instruments of redemption and deliverance, help and hope. And, like Moses, by nature we make excuses. I wonder if you've ever missed a moment that might have changed your life or that might have allowed you to be a part of something great God was doing in the world, simply because it felt inconvenient or frightening. Moses might well have resisted God's call and missed the amazing things God was about to do, and we would never have heard of the man. Instead, after arguing and debating and making excuses, Moses gave in and said, in essence, "Here I am Lord, send me."

God's call comes in many forms. On a daily basis God calls us to participate in his work of encouraging, blessing, challenging, liberating, and healing the world. Most often it happens in small ways. I was walking out of worship last week when I saw a man I had not seen before. I felt compelled to hurry and reach him before he left. I tapped him on the shoulder and said, "Hi, I just wanted to say that we're so glad you came to worship today. Thank you. I hope you come again." The man looked rather startled. We shook hands, and he turned and left.

I didn't think anything more about it until three days later, when I received a note from the man.

> I want to thank you for running after me following worship this weekend and for stopping to talk to me. I've been going through a difficult time in my personal life recently, and a friend strongly urged me to come to your church. I sat there in the service and felt like you were speaking to me. But as I was

leaving I thought, "This is such a big church. They couldn't care about me." Choking back the tears, I rushed off anticipating I would beat everyone else out. Then, right before I got to the door, I felt someone tap me on the shoulder. I turned around and could not believe it was you. In a service with over 2,000 people in attendance, you saw me, ran after me, and stopped me. I'm sorry I was rude and turned away. I was so utterly astounded that you had tapped me on the shoulder to thank me for coming.

That is a very small example of what I'm talking about, but it seems like this kind of thing happens every day when I'm paying attention. I'll feel nudged to visit someone in the hospital, or sit down and talk with someone, or give of my financial resources, or otherwise do something for someone else, and more often than not, I find myself in the midst of something God is doing. I've never had any huge burning bush experience, but I've had thousands of small experiences in which I felt that, for a particular person, I was God's instrument of encouragement, blessing, support, or help.

At every age and stage in life, God has a mission, a calling for us to fulfill. Our task is to pay attention to the burning bush, the whisper of the Spirit, the nudging inside. When God says, "Get going! I'm sending you!" we would do well to say, "Here I am, Lord, send me!"

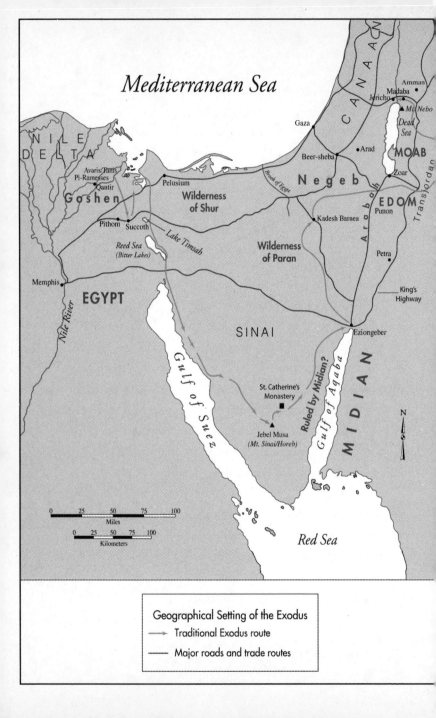

Geographical Setting of the Exodus
→ Traditional Exodus route
— Major roads and trade routes

3.

THE EXODUS

After exhausting his excuses to God, Moses finally capitulated and agreed to return to Egypt to confront Pharaoh. But first he traveled to Midian and spoke to his father-in-law, Jethro. Moses resigned from his work as Jethro's sheepherder and asked for Jethro's blessing on taking Moses' wife and sons with him to Egypt. Upon receiving that blessing, Moses began the journey back to Egypt.

The Journey to Egypt

Scripture tells us that, as Moses started the journey to Egypt, he placed his wife and children on a donkey.[1] Not far away, God spoke to Moses' biological brother, Aaron:

"Go into the desert to meet Moses." So he went, and Aaron
met him at God's mountain and greeted him with a kiss.
Moses told Aaron what the LORD had said about his mission
and all the signs that the LORD had told him to do.

(Exodus 4:27-28)

It appears that Moses and Aaron must have had contact over
the decades since Moses' birth, or at least since his flight to Midian.
Here God called Aaron and their sister, Miriam, to assist Moses in
discharging his mission. We'll see later in the story that God would
also call a man named Hur, as well as two younger men, Caleb and
Joshua, to support Moses in this important work. Aaron appears
to have held some influence among the Israelites in Egypt, possibly
serving as one of the "elders" of the people. When Aaron and Moses
arrived in the Delta, Aaron was able to call together the elders of
Israel to hear Moses describe his encounter with God and the
instructions he had received.

It would be easy to gloss over God's call to Aaron and Miriam
to assist Moses. But it reflects something important and consistent
about how God seems to work. Nearly always in Scripture when God
calls an individual to act, God also calls others to come alongside
and help. Moses had Aaron, Miriam, Hur, Joshua, and Caleb. David
had Jonathan, Joab, and a number of others at various times during
his long life. Jesus had the twelve disciples. And when Jesus sent his
followers out to minister to the multitudes, he sent them in pairs.
Paul had Barnabas, and later he had Silas, Timothy, Titus, and Luke.

Thinking of the men and women who have come alongside me
in ministry at the church I serve, I realize that most of what has
happened there has taken place because of them; they are selfless,
passionate, committed servants of God, and I thank God for them

daily. At some point, all of us will be called to serve as someone else's Aaron, helping others pursue the calling that God has placed on their lives. As we'll see, Aaron, Joshua, and Caleb's roles would be as critical as Moses' role in liberating the Israelite slaves and delivering them to the Promised Land.

Among the untold heroines in this story—untold because in the patriarchal world of the Bible, the work of women was seldom celebrated—was Zipporah, the wife of Moses. Consider the fact that Moses must have come in from tending sheep one evening and told Zipporah, "A God named I Am spoke to me through a burning bush today. He said we're to return to Egypt, to confront Pharaoh and demand that he release the Israelite slaves." It would be understandable if Zipporah, upon hearing this, had suggested that Moses had lost his mind. Instead she agreed to go, along with her children, on a journey that easily could have resulted in her husband's death and the enslavement of Zipporah and her children.

We have little information about Zipporah, but Exodus 4:24-26 preserves an interesting and perplexing story that I'm often asked about, one that illustrates her leadership and quick thinking. In Exodus 4:24 we read, concerning the journey back to Egypt: "On the way, at a place where they spent the night, the LORD met him and tried to kill him" (NRSV). It appears at first glance that, faced with the imminent death of her husband, Zipporah sprang into action, circumcising her son and then touching Moses with the foreskin, saying, "You are my bridegroom because of bloodshed." Upon hearing her words, God relented from killing Moses.

Another possible reading of the story is offered by Rabbi Jeffrey Cohen. He suggests that God was not threatening to kill Moses, but Moses' firstborn son. The reason for this was that Moses' son had not been circumcised as was commanded by God for all of Abraham's descendants. Cohen notes that in the previous verse, God had sworn to kill Pharaoh's firstborn if he refused to allow the Israelites to go to the Sinai to worship. Thus, the threat to Moses' firstborn was in a sense an illustration for Moses of the warning he was to deliver to Pharaoh. This interpretation is possible in that the Hebrew doesn't specify whether it was Moses or Moses' son whom God was seeking to kill.[2]

Whatever the interpretation, the passage shows that Zipporah, though seldom mentioned in the Torah, was no wallflower. She was a woman of courage, wisdom, and action who fearlessly protected her family. Zipporah's important role can be added to those of the two midwives, Moses' mother, Pharaoh's daughter, and Miriam—other women whose bravery made the story of Moses possible.

Pharaoh of the Exodus

In the introduction to this book I mentioned the debate about the timing of the Exodus—the liberation of the Israelite slaves. While some conservative scholars suggest that the Exodus took place during the reign of Thutmose III or Ahmenetop II in the middle of the fifteenth century B.C., many scholars place the Exodus in the thirteenth century before Christ, during the reign of Pharaoh Ramesses II.

This latter dating approach fits nicely with the mention in Exodus 1:11 of the city of Ramesses, which only came to be known by that name during the reign of Ramesses II.[3] This city, Exodus tells us, was built by Israelite slaves. Egyptian history tells us that Ramesses II built it to be a new and glorious northern capital for Egypt. The

Ramesses II enthroned at the Luxor Temple

construction of the city was begun under Ramesses II's father, Seti I, but only completed under his son. It was built on one of the branches of the Nile in the Delta and became an important city owing to its proximity to Egypt's breadbasket and to the important trade routes by land to the east and by sea to the north and west.

Knowing the timing of the Exodus is not critical in order to understand the story, but it is easy to imagine Ramesses II as Pharaoh of the Exodus, and he adds to the drama of the story thanks to what we know of him through Egyptian archaeology.

Ramesses II was born in 1303 B.C. and died in 1213, living to the age of ninety. He ruled over Egypt for sixty-five years. Known as Ramesses the Great, he ruled during a golden age for Egypt. He was responsible for massive building projects across Egypt, on a scale Egypt had seldom seen before or since. Ramesses II had thousands of statues of himself erected across Egypt marking his building projects and serving as expressions of his power and his sense of his own greatness.

I remember visiting a pastor's office years ago. Sitting there, I couldn't help but notice that behind him was a giant portrait of himself. On his other wall were five more portraits of himself in various poses, and on another wall two more. I left feeling that the portraits had told me something about the man's ego. In the same way, the sheer number of statues and bas reliefs of Ramesses II likely tells us something about this pharaoh.

Traveling across Egypt, you can see temples dedicated to Ramesses II and statuary of his likeness, along with hundreds of bas reliefs of battles he purportedly fought in. You can visit his grave in the Valley of the Kings near Luxor, and, if you go to the Egyptian Museum in Cairo, you can actually see his mummified body including his

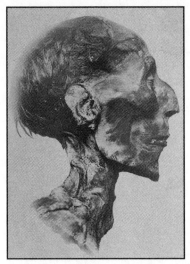

Image of mummified Ramesses II

carefully manicured fingernails and even the hair on his head! Mummies of his father and grandfather are nearby.

Ramesses II was likely the most powerful man on the face of the planet at the time Moses and Zipporah, their sons Gershom and Eliezar, and Moses' brother Aaron were on their way to meet him. Can you imagine the sheepherders Moses and Aaron approaching the royal palace in Pi-Ramesses? The fact that they were able to see Pharaoh at all may point to the important place Aaron played among the Israelites, though it is also possible that Moses' earlier position in the royal family opened the doors for this meeting.

Initially Moses and Aaron were not asking for Pharaoh to free the slaves, only to let the people go to Mount Sinai to worship God. Nevertheless, from Pharaoh's perspective their request would have seemed absurd. If we were to think of their meeting with Pharaoh as a boxing match, in one corner we'd have an eighty-year-old stuttering sheepherder and his eighty-three-year-old brother; and in the other corner would be the colossus of Egypt, the most powerful man on the planet, the awesome and glorious Ramesses the Great!

Bearing in mind the idea of a boxing match, let's find out what happened when they met in Exodus 5:1-2:

Moses and Aaron went to Pharaoh and said, "This is what the LORD, Israel's God, says: 'Let my people go so that they can hold a festival for me in the desert.'" But Pharaoh said, "Who is this LORD whom I'm supposed to obey by letting Israel go? I don't know this LORD, and I certainly won't let Israel go."

This is masterful storytelling. Did you hear Pharaoh's prideful roar when he asked, "Who is this LORD?" Maybe you noticed the statement of self-condemnation that must have delighted Israelites listening to the story: "I don't know this LORD." Pharaoh himself was semidivine, according to Egypt's religion, and he acted as intermediary between the gods and humanity, but he had not heard of Yahweh, nor did he show respect for Yahweh.

What followed this first meeting was an epic battle between the all-powerful Pharaoh and the shepherd Moses. But it was more than that. It was a battle between Yahweh, Israel's God, and the entire pantheon of Egyptian gods and goddesses.

Initially, Moses and Aaron were asking Pharaoh to let the Israelites travel into the Sinai to worship their God. In response, Pharaoh instructed the Israelites' slavemasters,

"Don't supply the people with the straw they need to make bricks like you did before. Let them go out and gather the straw for themselves. But still make sure that they produce the same number of bricks as they made before. Don't reduce the number! They are weak and lazy, and that's why they cry, 'Let us go and offer sacrifices to our God.' Make the men's work so hard that it's all they can do, and they can't focus on these empty lies."

(Exodus 5:7-9)

Mud and straw brick construction that could have been from the time of Moses

It is not difficult to picture this story when walking across archaeological sites of ancient Egypt. Bricks made of mud and straw can be seen at so many of these sites. In the buildings from the time of Ramesses, millions of these mud bricks are still in place. As I touched them and picked them up, I couldn't help but wonder if the bricks had been made by the hands of the Israelite slaves.

Visiting the City of Ramesses

Among the places I wanted to see while walking in Moses' footsteps was the city of Ramesses, or Pi-Ramesses (House of Ramesses) as it was officially called, which was constructed by the Israelite slaves on one of the main branches of the Nile River in the Delta. That city has been described by archaeologists who have explored what's left of it as the Venice of ancient Egypt. It had multiple lakes, canals, a massive

Ruins of the temple at Tanis

temple, and magnificent palaces. If the Exodus occurred during the reign of Ramesses II, then this city would have been the setting for the stories of Exodus 5 through 12.

When going to visit the remains of Pi-Ramesses, one has to decide which of two archaeological sites to visit. The first site is the actual location of Pi-Ramesses during the time of Ramesses II, a place called Qantir. But two hundred years after the time of Moses, silt had filled in the branch of the Nile on which Pi-Ramesses was built, and so the city was relocated, stone by stone, building by building, eighteen miles north along another branch of the Nile to a site that today is called Tanis. Since we didn't have time to visit both sites before the sun went down, and since the Egyptians left very little of Pi-Ramesses at Qantir, we opted to walk the ancient streets of Tanis, the secondary location, where we saw the remains of buildings that the Israelite slaves had constructed for Ramesses II, but which had been relocated to this site.

It was no small task getting to Tanis. Few have heard of this site, unless perhaps they've watched the movie *Raiders of the Lost Ark*,

Giant statue of Ramesses II at Tanis

whose setting was said to be Tanis, where the film's fictional story depicted the Nazis' discovery of the Ark of the Covenant. Of course, this never happened, but the city has yielded many amazing ancient Egyptian treasures in tombs that were found undisturbed there. These discoveries, though not as well known, were comparable in importance to the great treasures from the tomb of King Tutankhamun in the Valley of the Kings. Much of the ancient city remains buried underground, and limited funds have kept it from being explored further.

As we drove up to the main entrance, the archaeological site appeared abandoned. The gates were chained, their locks rusted. No one seemed to have keys. An alternative road to the site was blocked with debris. We finally exited our vehicle, hopped in the back of a pickup truck with the Egyptian soldiers who accompanied us, and made our way to the site. A couple of houses there are kept for visiting archaeological teams. A lone archaeologist came out from one of the houses and agreed to give us a tour.

We entered the ancient city through one of its original gates, which had been erected in place over three thousand years ago. We passed among giant statues of Ramesses II that bore silent witness to the king we'd traveled hours to meet. Spread out before us, and the focus of much archaeological work on the site, was the massive temple of Amun-Ra, the chief among Egypt's gods in the New Kingdom period, the Zeus of the Egyptian pantheon. The site is one of the largest temple complexes not only in ancient Egypt, but in the world. The name of Ramesses II, builder of Pi-Ramesses, appears on stones throughout the temple.

The Battle Is Drawn: The Ten Plagues

Following Moses' initial request that Pharaoh let the people go, Pharaoh commanded that the Israelites would henceforth be forced to collect their own straw to make mud bricks, while maintaining the same daily quotas—an impossibility, complained the Israelite leaders bitterly. Moses and Aaron, far from delivering the Israelites, had just made their lives harder. Moses cried out to God:

> "My Lord, why have you abused this people? Why did you send me for this? Ever since I first came to Pharaoh to speak in your name, he has abused this people. And you've done absolutely nothing to rescue your people."

> The LORD replied to Moses, "Now you will see what I'll do to Pharaoh. In fact, he'll be so eager to let them go that he'll drive them out of his land by force."

> (Exodus 5:22-23; 6:1)

The Ten Plagues of Egypt

1 Water Turns to Blood

2 Frogs

3 Lice

4 Flies

5 Sick Cattle

6 Boils

7 Fire/Hail

8 Locusts

9 Darkness

10 Death of Firstborn

What follows is the story of the ten plagues. There are several ways to interpret the story. One way is to read it straight up, with the plagues occurring exactly as recorded in Exodus (an extreme of the "maximalist" view we learned of earlier). A second way to read the story of the plagues is to recognize that many of the plagues appear to have been naturally occurring phenomena that at times afflicted ancient Egypt (and are still seen from time to time today). In this second view, God used these natural events to accomplish God's purposes. In a moment we'll explore a third way of making sense of the plagues, but first let's consider the idea that these plagues were naturally occurring phenomena whose timing was orchestrated by God.

In the first plague, the waters in the Nile and across Egypt were turned to blood. Next, the frogs left the Nile and covered the ground.

Then gnats or lice begin to swarm, followed by flies, and soon diseases began killing the livestock. Before long, people developed boils on their skin. Next, fire and hail damaged the crops, followed by locusts, then darkness, and finally the deaths of the firstborn.

All the plagues seem similar to phenomena that sometimes occur in nature. Scientists have suggested that a particular type of algae caused the red color of the Nile and other waters; when such blooms occur they often are called "red tides." In the summer of 2016, for example, Iran's Lake Urmia changed from a deep green to a blood red owing to algal blooms. (The change was visible on satellite images that can be seen on the Internet.)

These algal blooms can be toxic for the fish and other sea life, which is consistent with the description in Exodus 7:21: "The fish in the Nile died, and the Nile began to stink so that the Egyptians couldn't drink water from the Nile."

The subsequent plagues may have resulted from the first. Frogs left the Nile and covered the land. The dead fish and dying frogs could have provided a perfect breeding ground for the "lice" (or gnats or fleas or mosquitoes—the meaning of the Hebrew word is unclear). Next came the flies; no surprise there either. Then the livestock began to die—cattle, camels, goats, sheep, horses. This too makes sense, as the biting insects could have spread disease. After that, the people became sick with painful lesions on their skin, a condition that could have been caused by swarms of biting insects that transmitted disease.

The next plague consisted of hail and lightning that destroyed crops and trees. I come from Kansas, and this plague almost feels like home! Every spring we have hailstorms. I've held golf ball-size hailstones, and I've seen pictures of softball-size hailstones that fell in Texas. (Everything is bigger in Texas!) Hailstones, whether large or small, can destroy crops, trees, and dwellings.

Try Googling locust videos, and you'll find this plague still occurring today, destroying crops as it did in Egypt. Interestingly, a plague of locusts that struck the American Midwest in July 1931 was described as being of "biblical proportions." Three years later, conditions in the heartland led to the Dust Bowl, an ecological disaster caused by wind erosion. When a teacher in Oklahoma, my great-aunt Celia Bell Yoder lived through the Dust Bowl. She once described a terrible dust storm that turned day to night. She crowded the handful of children from her one-room schoolhouse into her Ford, noting that the children could not see their houses from the road where she dropped them off. Is this what the Egyptians experienced in their plague of darkness?

Finally, and most dramatically, the firstborn children of the Egyptians and their firstborn livestock were struck down. This could have been the result of a pestilence that began with the death of the fish and frogs, and which was spread to humans by the insects.

Were Moses' plagues a supernatural judgment of God upon the Egyptians or were they a recollection of actual plagues that struck Egypt from time to time but which were used by God? It's hard to know for sure. But there is a third way of reading the story.

Some, rightly I think, have seen in the plagues a bit of satire. The battle was not simply between an eighty-year-old shepherd and the powerful pharaoh; it was also between the God of Israel and the gods of Egypt.

Hapi, the god of the Nile, often portrayed as a pair representing the upper and lower Nile

The first plague, turning the Nile and the other waters to blood so they could not give life, was a way of showing God's control over the Nile. In Egyptian mythology the god of the Nile was called Hapi (often portrayed as a pair of figures). Hapi was crucial to sustaining of life in Egypt. But in this first plague, the God of Israel overpowered Hapi, the god of the Nile.

In the second plague, the frogs climbed out of the river and became a nuisance. Heket was a goddess in Egypt portrayed as a frog. Soon the Egyptians had come to despise the frogs and they began to die off—another act of judgment against Egypt's gods.

Likewise, the death of cattle in the fifth plague may have indicated God's power over the Egyptian goddess Hathor, who was often portrayed as a cow.

Hathor, the goddess portrayed as a cow

Where we see satire most dramatically is in the ninth plague, when the sun was blotted out. Remember that Ramesses' and Moses' names had a common root: Moses meant "son of," which without a prefix meant Son of No One; while Ramesses' name meant Son of Ra (Ra being the sun god). In this battle between the eighty-year-old stuttering Son of No One and the powerful Son of Ra the sun god, Moses' God, Yahweh, defeated Pharaoh's sun god, causing utter darkness.

Here's the point: Yahweh demonstrated in dramatic fashion, one by one, that the gods of Pharaoh and the Egyptians were impotent deities—they were not gods at all. This is captured in Numbers 33:4 where, reflecting on the last of the plagues, the writer notes, "The LORD also executed judgments against their gods."

Amun-Ra, the chief deity of Egypt, who also controls the sun

As I pondered the ten plagues, I thought of modern-day versions of them, where devastation occurs, leaving those in their wake asking serious questions about the meaning of life and realizing that the gods we tend to worship are powerless. The Great Recession of 2008 was, in its way, one of those modern-day plagues. Day after day we watched as the markets dropped. Major American companies disappeared from the economic landscape—companies previously thought "too big to fail." In one of the essays on Exodus in his excellent book, *Covenant & Conversation*, Rabbi Jonathan Sacks captures the message of that modern-day plague in these words: "When money rules, we remember the price of things and forget the value of things."[4]

Before moving to the climax of the story, it's important to address one of several disturbing ideas in the account of the plagues. Scripture says that for each of the first five plagues, Pharaoh "hardened his heart" (Exodus 8:15 NRSV) and would not let the people go; but when we come to the second five plagues, we read that "the LORD hardened the heart of Pharaoh" (Exodus 9:12 NRSV, *emphasis added*) and kept him from relenting. The word *harden* usually means to strengthen or fortify, and some think that God simply gave Pharaoh courage to continue to be the pharaoh that he was: brash, unrelenting, and certain that he didn't need to listen to anyone or anything. This interpretation is challenging to those, including me, who believe that God gives us free will.

One interesting term used when Pharaoh is said to have hardened his own heart is the Hebrew word *kabed*, meaning to make heavy. I was struck by the connection between the heaviness of Pharaoh's heart and his own beliefs concerning what would happen to him at his death. Those beliefs were part of every pharaoh's education.

From the moment pharaohs were enthroned, regardless of age, they began working with an architect to design their burial chamber. In the centuries long before Ramesses, these burial chambers were pyramids. But by the time of Ramesses the chambers were below-ground mausoleums, as I described in the previous chapter. The burial preparations and burial chambers were all intended to help the pharaoh's journey to the next life, where they would be deified. Detailed instructions about passing to the next life would be shown on the coffin, on the walls, sometimes on the linens that wrapped the pharaoh's body, and (by the time of Ramesses II) on some of the scrolls in the burial chamber. For the pharaohs, this was their transition to deity. These instructions were collectively known as the Book of the Dead.[5]

Jackal-headed god Anubis, who weighed the pharaoh's heart before allowing passage to the afterlife

The Book of the Dead, Spell 125, depicted the famous "weighing of the heart." In this account, the dead pharaoh was taken to Osiris by the jackal-headed god Anubis. Before the pharaoh and Osiris stood a scale, with an ostrich feather on one side of the scale representing the goddess Maat, the embodiment of truth and justice, and with the pharaoh's heart on the other side of the scale. The weighing of the heart ultimately showed whether the pharaoh was just or unjust. If the heart was too heavy, a terrifying beast called Ammit stood by to devour it and put a final end to the pharaoh's hopes of passing into the afterlife.

Thus we can see that in the story of Moses, the emphasis on Pharaoh's heart being hardened (becoming heavy)—whether Pharaoh did this to himself or God did it to him—might have been a satirical way of pointing out the impact of Pharaoh's cruelty on his own chances of everlasting life.

The Passover

Let's return to the final plague, the climax of this epic battle, in which God's judgment would be poured upon Egypt, and God would deliver Israel from death, oppression, and slavery. In delivering the Israelites, God would make them his covenant people and lead them to the Promised Land.

Moses told the Israelites to prepare for the final plague by slaughtering a lamb and roasting and eating it as a family. They were to take lamb's blood and, using a branch of hyssop (an herb used by Egyptian priests in rituals of purification), brush the blood on the doorposts of their homes. That night, God would send an angel of death throughout Egypt, taking the life of every firstborn child and the firstborn of every flock. But when the angel came to a home with the blood of the lamb on its doorposts, death would pass over this home. Hence the night would be commemorated by Israelites as the Passover. This final plague would drive Egypt to her knees and would force Pharaoh to let the Israelite slaves go free.

Exodus records what happened that night:

> At midnight the LORD struck down all the first offspring
> in the land of Egypt.... A terrible cry of agony rang out
> across Egypt because every house had someone in it who had
> died. Then Pharaoh called Moses and Aaron that night and
> said, "Get up! Get away from my people, both you and the
> Israelites! Go!"
>
> (Exodus 12:29-31)

The story describes God's victory over Egypt's gods and over the semidivine Pharaoh, while visiting judgment on the Egyptian people for decades of oppression of the Israelites. God rescued Israel, whom he called "my firstborn" in Exodus 4:22 (NRSV), by taking the lives of Egypt's firstborn.

But there is also something deeply disturbing about the story if you read it as entirely historical. God sent an angel of death to slaughter infants, children, and any who were firstborn, including "the oldest child of the servant woman by the millstones, and all the first offspring of the animals" (Exodus 11:5)—over one hundred thousand people and thousands of animals.[6] This action seems inconsistent with a God who is "compassionate and merciful, very patient, full of great loyalty and faithfulness" (Exodus 34:6).

There are several ways of thinking about this final plague that might help us in making sense of the story's moral tension. For the minimalist, the Exodus and the plagues are simply an epic story written hundreds of years after it occurred with limited historical value. For the maximalist, the story as written is a more or less accurate representation of history. Many would see, as the author of Exodus does, the death of the Egyptian firstborn as the just judgment of God upon the Egyptians.

My own view, as previously noted, is somewhere between these two positions. I believe the Exodus was written as Israel's epic story, but it does not reflect a journalist's account of the events. The story was rooted in historical events that took place leading up to the release of the Israelite slaves, but there was license in how the story was interpreted and told. To repeat the earlier analogy, if the Exodus story as told in the Torah were a film, it would be "based upon actual events" rather than a documentary. Reading the story in this way allows us to recognize that this or that detail might have been added by the storyteller to heighten the tension, to simplify and summarize a more complex reality, or to make a point. But the arc of the story occurred broadly as described.

If we view the plagues as a cascading series of naturally occurring events that God initiated to release his people from bondage, then it seems possible that the death of the firstborn was the natural climax of the earlier plagues. Consider that the plague of the boils sounds very much like bacterial epidemics that have afflicted humans throughout history. I think of the Black Death that struck Europe in the fourteenth century, resulting in the death of over fifty million people.[7]

Another possible explanation for the final plague is the *Bacillus anthracis* bacterium, which causes the anthrax infection. Anthrax, among humans, can be spread through contact with infected livestock. Thus the boils of the sixth plague could have been the direct result of handling or consuming the infected livestock from the fifth plague. Given that firstborn males may have been most likely to be responsible for tending the sick livestock, one might imagine they could have been disproportionately affected and consequently could have died—hence the last plague being remembered as the death of the firstborn.

In any event, the impact of these successive plagues, particularly the last, was for Pharaoh and the Egyptians to beg the Israelites to leave their land, and even to help them as they left.

Following their liberation, God commanded the Israelites to commemorate the Passover event annually with a meal. And so each year, in the Passover Seder, Jews reenact and retell their story so they will never forget that they once were slaves but by the power and grace of God were set free. Every element of the meal symbolizes some part of the story: the bitterness of slavery, the plagues, the

Passover lamb, the unleavened bread that didn't have time to rise as the Israelites hurried to leave Egypt. At that meal, four cups of wine are to be drunk. A small portion of the wine is spilled at the telling of each plague, with two portions or drops spilled with the last plague. Some interpret the spilling of the wine as a recognition of the pain that the plagues inflicted on the Egyptians, with the double portion spilled as a reminder of the terrible price paid in the final plague for the Israelites' freedom.

In reading the story or experiencing the Passover Seder, we should feel the pain of that night alongside the joy of liberation. And we must also remember the decades of oppression and pain inflicted upon the Israelites by Pharaoh and the Egyptians. Generation after generation of injustice, oppression, and death led to the day of liberation.

Early Christians saw in the story of the Passover a foreshadowing of the Christian gospel. In the Passover story, Egypt's firstborn children died because of the sins of Egypt. In the gospel, Jesus is God's "firstborn" (Hebrews 1:6) who would die for the sins of the human race.

The early church saw the slaughter of the lambs used at Passover as prefiguring the death of Jesus, speaking of "Christ our Passover lamb" (1 Corinthians 5:7). The blood of the Passover lambs was shed, not as a sacrifice for sin, but as a way of protecting the Israelite firstborn children from the plague of death. The Passover lamb was pivotal in the dramatic story of God's delivering the Israelites from slavery, and the ritual of the Passover Seder came to be associated with liberation from slavery and from death.

The idea of the Passover lamb slaughtered to protect the Israelites from death, and the mention later in the Torah of animals being sacrificed to atone for sin, were conflated in the Gospel of John when John described Jesus as "the Lamb of God who takes away the sin of the world" (John 1:29). Near the end of his Gospel, John again connects the Passover lamb with the lamb shed for sin. He does this in his mention of hyssop. The Israelites were instructed to use the hyssop plant to spread the lamb's blood on their doorposts, and Moses would later use hyssop branches in various rituals of purification for the people (see Leviticus 14 and Numbers 19). So John introduces a hyssop branch into the story of Jesus' crucifixion, noting that as Jesus hung on the cross, someone took a sponge, dipped it into sour wine, attached it to a hyssop branch, and lifted the branch to Jesus' lips so he could draw a drink from the sponge (John 19:29).

For Jews, the central saving act of God on their behalf was the night when God liberated the Israelites from slavery in Egypt, claimed them as his own people, and began their journey to the Promised Land, and this night is commemorated annually in the Passover Seder. For Christians, God's central saving act for all humanity was the death and resurrection of Christ. It was not by accident that Jesus' last supper with his disciples, the evening before his crucifixion, was a Passover Seder.[8] At that meal, Jesus reinterpreted the eating of unleavened bread and the drinking of wine. Breaking the bread, he told his disciples, "This is my body given for you; do this in remembrance of me"; and taking the cup, he said, "This cup is the new covenant in my blood, which is poured out for you" (Luke 22:19-20 NIV).

The Parting of the Sea

Following the plague of the firstborn, Pharaoh released the Israelites, and they departed Pi-Ramesses in the middle of the night. Exodus 13:17-18 notes,

> When Pharaoh let the people go, God didn't lead them by way of the land of the Philistines, even though that was the shorter route. God thought, If the people have to fight and face war, they will run back to Egypt. So God led the people by the roundabout way of the Reed Sea desert.

In a strange turn of events, God commanded Moses to lead the people to set up camp in front of the Reed Sea. The Reed Sea is the literal reading of the Hebrew that is usually translated as "Red Sea." As you can see on the map at the beginning of this chapter, the Red Sea is farther to the south, while the Reed Sea was likely one of the lakes between the Mediterranean Sea to the north and the Red Sea to the south that in modern times have been bisected by the Suez Canal. Lake Timsah and the Greater and Lesser Bitter Lakes are in the general vicinity where Moses and the Israelites may have traveled. It is possible that the crossing of the sea occurred at one of these locations or at one of the shallow marshy lakes in the same general area that have since dried up.

We traveled to this area to see one of the lakes that remains. We arrived at our lakeside hotel in Ismalia after dark, following a long day of exploring and travel. After a brief meal we collapsed into bed, unable to see much from our hotel windows by night. But the next morning we watched the sun come up over Lake Timsah, also called Crocodile Lake, and wondered if this might have been the very place

Lake Timsah, possible location of the Reed Sea crossing

where Moses and the Israelites made camp before God's final victory on their behalf.[9]

That day we spent exploring the shoreline of Lake Timsah, recognizing that this is only one of several possible locations for the crossing of the Reed Sea. We stopped to walk alongside the lake, to watch the waters lapping the shore, and to imagine the dramatic events that happened here, or somewhere nearby. From there we could see the large ships passing along the east side of the lake through the Suez Canal.

To the Israelites, it must have seemed an odd place to camp. To the east was a marshy lake. To the west was Pharaoh's Egypt. If for any reason Pharaoh should come after them, they would be trapped. But surely, they must have hoped, that would not happen.

Pharaoh, hearing that the slaves had camped near the lake and now regretting his decision to let such a massive labor force go free,

Bas-relief of Ramesses II in his chariot at the Battle of Kadesh

decided to go after them and to retrieve them as Egypt's slaves. We read in Exodus 14:6-7, "So he sent for his chariot and took his army with him. He took six hundred elite chariots and all of Egypt's other chariots with captains on all of them."

It was the elite chariots that made Pharaoh's army so imposing. These were the latest in military technology. Examples of Pharaoh riding his chariot into battle can be seen in bas reliefs on the sides of many Egyptian temples that were built or expanded by Ramesses II. Amazingly, at the Egyptian Museum in Cairo you can see actual chariots used shortly before the time of the Exodus, which were wonderfully preserved in King Tut's tomb.

Exodus 14:9 notes, "The Egyptians, including all of Pharaoh's horse-drawn chariots, his cavalry, and his army, chased them and caught up with them as they were camped by the sea." Up to this point in the story, it had been Pharaoh and his gods with whom God had battled. Now, God was about to display his power against the greatest military power on earth at the time.

We know from the battle of Kadesh, in which Ramesses II fought against the Hittites, that Egypt had several thousand chariots in addition to the six hundred elite chariots. The chariots were lighter and more advanced than those of other nations. One modern engineer described them as the Formula One racers of their time. Two horses would draw the chariot, which was piloted by one warrior while another, using Egypt's advanced composite bows, fired at their enemies from a distance. As the charioteers drew closer, swords and spears were used.

It is not difficult to imagine what the mostly unarmed Israelites were feeling as they saw the dust from Pharaoh's chariots in the distance.

> The Israelites were terrified and cried out to the LORD. They said to Moses, "Weren't there enough graves in Egypt that you took us away to die in the desert? What have you done to us by bringing us out of Egypt like this? Didn't we tell you the same thing in Egypt? 'Leave us alone! Let us work for the Egyptians!' It would have been better for us to work for the Egyptians than to die in the desert."

> But Moses said to the people, "Don't be afraid. Stand your ground, and watch the LORD rescue you today. The Egyptians you see today you will never ever see again. The LORD will fight for you. You just keep still."

> (Exodus 14:10-14)

Nightfall came, and the Egyptians made camp opposite the Israelites. God commanded Moses to lift his staff over the water.

That night a strong east wind came blowing across the water toward the Israelites, and when morning came they found the water pushed back by the wind on either side of a path that had been cleared through the middle of the sea. Using the path, the Israelites walked through the water as if on dry land. The Egyptians tried to follow, but their chariots appeared to become stuck in the seabed, slowing them down. When the Israelites arrived on the other side of the sea, God commanded Moses to stretch back his staff over the waters. When he did, the waters returned, covering the Egyptian army and charioteers. The finest army in the land was utterly destroyed.

Some will point out that the lakes in this region were, and continue to be, very shallow, and that's true. As a result, what actually happened may not have resembled the scene as captured in films, with walls of water hundreds of feet high. Today the lakes range in depth from just a few feet at the shallowest to thirty-six feet at the deepest part of the Great Bitter Lake. Whatever happened, regardless of how deep the water, Pharaoh's army was defeated, not by the Israelites but by God himself.

As the Israelites stood watching this scene unfold, they were undoubtedly filled with awe. They had been utterly delivered from Pharaoh and the greatest military power of the day. In response, Moses and the Israelites composed and sang a song. Here are some of its words, found in Exodus 15:1-5.

> I will sing to the LORD, for an overflowing victory!
>> Horse and rider he threw into the sea!
> The LORD is my strength and my power;
>> he has become my salvation.
> This is my God, whom I will praise,
>> the God of my ancestors, whom I will acclaim.

The LORD is a warrior;
　　the LORD is his name.
Pharaoh's chariots and his army he hurled into the sea;
　　his elite captains were sunk in the Reed Sea.
The deep sea covered them;
　　they sank into the deep waters like a stone.

A rabbi friend describing the Passover Seder noted, "This is our defining story. If you are a Jew, you've got to get this. It defines who we are as a people. We were slaves. God saw our suffering. God delivered us and made us his own. This is our story."

When God chose a people with whom he would have a special covenant relationship, he selected a group that was oppressed and enslaved. He delivered them by his "mighty right hand." There was nothing they could have done to deliver themselves. There's a word that describes this kind of salvation: *grace*. It was salvation that the Israelites did nothing to deserve; it was purely an act of God's kindness, mercy, and love.

What does the story mean for Christians? It means that God cares about the nobodies! It means that God will ultimately defeat the arrogant, prideful, and cruel. It means that God sees our suffering, and God will deliver us. It means that we don't have to remain enslaved to the things that bind us. God can set us free.

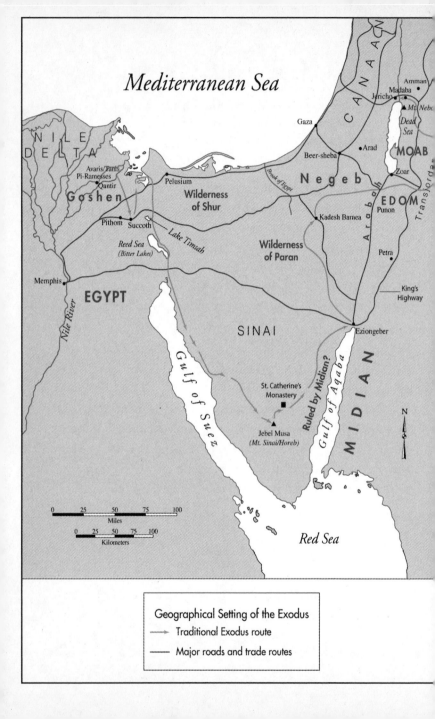

Mediterranean Sea

CANAAN

Amman
Madaba
Jericho
Mt. Nebo
Dead Sea

Gaza

Beer-sheba
Arad
MOAB
Zoar
EDOM

NILE DELTA

Avaris/Tanis
Pi-Ramesses
Qantir
Goshen
Pelusium

Wilderness of Shur

Brook of Egypt

N e g e b

Punon
Transjordan

Pithom
Succoth
Lake Timsah
Reed Sea
(Bitter Lakes)

Kadesh Barnea

Wilderness of Paran

Petra

Memphis

EGYPT

King's Highway

Nile River

SINAI

Eziongeber

Gulf of Suez

St. Catherine's Monastery

Ruled by Midian?

Gulf of Aqaba

MIDIAN

Jebel Musa
(Mt. Sinai/Horeb)

N

0   25   50   75   100
Miles

0   25   50   75   100
Kilometers

Red Sea

Geographical Setting of the Exodus
→ Traditional Exodus route
— Major roads and trade routes

4.

THE TEN COMMANDMENTS

Following God's dramatic victory over the Egyptian army at the Reed Sea, the Israelites sang, worshiped, and feasted as they celebrated their newfound freedom. Then they followed Moses as he began the journey back to Mount Sinai where he had first encountered God. They would take three months to make the 190-mile journey, and once there they would remain camped at Sinai for the next eleven months.

During those eleven months Moses would repeatedly climb Mount Sinai, and God would descend upon the mountaintop to meet him, often in dramatic fashion with smoke, thunder, and lightning. At these meetings God and Moses conversed "face-to-face, like two people talking to each other" (Exodus 33:11). Moses would then bring down from the mountain God's commands for the people, including the ordering of their religious and civil life. Mount Sinai is the setting for Exodus 19–40, all of Leviticus, and Numbers 1–10. In these passages Mount Sinai is referred to in various ways, including Mount Horeb (though in a handful of places this name seems to refer to a separate mountain) and often simply "the mountain of God" (NRSV).

Centuries after the time of Moses, in a period of great adversity, the prophet Elijah returned to Mount Sinai to ascend as Moses had done, in the hope of meeting God. Today thousands of pilgrims each year hike Mount Sinai, also hoping to meet God. This was our hope as well as we crossed under the Suez Canal in the Ahmed Hamdi Tunnel and began our journey south on the Ras Sedr Road, on our way to the mountain of God.

Visiting Sinai

If today's Mount Sinai is the biblical Mount Sinai (as noted earlier, no one can say for sure), then the route we drove, south along the eastern shore of the Gulf of Suez, stood a fair chance of being the route the Israelites traveled as Moses led them to the place where he'd encountered God. Modern roadways typically follow the same routes used in the ancient world, because travelers at that time, like today, sought the fastest, easiest, and safest paths from Point A to Point B.

We traveled 120 miles south by southeast on Ras Sedr Road, with the Gulf of Suez to our right and the Sinai Desert to our left, before we reached the road to the interior of Sinai. Along the way we passed a handful of small towns located on the coast, but for the most part

View of the Plain of Rest from St. Catherine's Monastery

the journey today looks the way it likely did to the Israelites long ago. Turning east on St. Catherine's Road, we left the sea behind, beginning our journey up and into the heart of the southern Sinai Peninsula and its high mountain range. Soon we were surrounded by mountains on both sides, some rising as high as eight thousand feet. The terrain was breathtaking that afternoon as we wound our way some seventy miles through the beautiful landscape.

We finally arrived at the town of St. Catherine, just a few miles from Mount Sinai, beneath which St. Catherine's Monastery is located. The town, with a population of more than four thousand residents, is at an elevation of 5,200 feet above sea level. A few modest hotels provide places for pilgrims to get a meal and bed down for a few hours of sleep before hiking the mountain. Many pilgrims awake several hours before dawn to hike Mount Sinai, so they can watch the sunrise from the mountaintop.

We were there in February, and I had assumed the Sinai would be warm that time of year. In many places it is, but the mountains around St. Catherine's boast the coldest temperatures in Egypt. It is one of the only places in all of Egypt where snow occasionally falls. The night we stayed there, the temperature was in the low thirties.

The Exodus account tells us that

> On exactly the third-month anniversary of the Israelites'
> leaving the land of Egypt, they came into the Sinai desert.
> They traveled from Rephidim, came into the Sinai desert,
> and set up camp there. Israel camped there in front of the
> mountain while Moses went up to God.
>
> (Exodus 19:1-3)

A large valley at the base of Mount Sinai is called the Plain of el-Raha, "the Plain of Rest." Here the Israelites were said to have camped for nearly a year. Again, the events described in Exodus 19–40, all of Leviticus, and Numbers 1–10 are set here. Walking across the plain, and later looking down at the plain from above, it was easy to picture thousands of Israelite tents pitched here. It was here, according to tradition, that Moses forty years earlier had met Zipporah, his wife. And it was here, just months before leading the Israelites to this place, that Moses while grazing his father-in-law's flock had heard the voice of God speak to him from the burning bush.

Powerful Encounters

Towering above the valley are three mountain peaks, but the one that most people climb is referred to by those who live in the region as Jebel Musa—the Mountain of Moses. It is not the tallest of the three peaks, though it is shorter only by a few hundred feet. Pictures don't do it justice. I had seen many photos in the past that tended to make the mountain appear smaller than it is. Its craggy form is unobstructed by trees. Little vegetation grows on the sides of this mountain. But it was here, tradition tells us, that God met with Moses and entered into a covenant with the slaves he had just set free.

> The LORD called to him from the mountain, "This is what
> you should say to Jacob's household and declare to the
> Israelites: You saw what I did to the Egyptians, and how I
> lifted you up on eagles' wings and brought you to me. So now,
> if you faithfully obey me and stay true to my covenant, you
> will be my most precious possession out of all the peoples,
> since the whole earth belongs to me. You will be a kingdom
> of priests for me and a holy nation. These are the words you
> should say to the Israelites."
>
> (Exodus 19:3-6)

This important passage was meant to shape the self-understanding of the Israelite people. It captured God's purpose in delivering the Israelites and God's mission for his people. God would enter into a covenant with them, and they with him. He would consider them his most precious possession, and they would become a kingdom of priests who represented God and mediated God's word, God's purposes, and God's grace to the rest of the world.

Christians will be interested to note that the terms of this special relationship are echoed in 1 Peter 2:9-10, which appropriates God's words in Exodus to describe the missional identity of Jesus' followers:

> You are a chosen race, a royal priesthood, a holy nation, a
> people who are God's own possession. You have become this

people so that you may speak of the wonderful acts of the one
who called you out of darkness into his amazing light. Once
you weren't a people, but now you are God's people. Once
you hadn't received mercy, but now you have received mercy.[1]

There are so many points at which Moses' story parallels the
Gospel story of Jesus, points where the Gospel writers seemed to
intend for their readers to note the allusions to the Exodus stories. In
Moses' story, it was "on the third day" that God's glory was revealed
on Mount Sinai; the Gospel accounts tell us it was "on the third day"
that the stone sealing Christ's tomb was cast aside and Christ rose,
revealing God's glory and God's power over evil, sin, and death.

In the Torah, Moses went up on the mountain to receive the Law;
in Matthew, Jesus went up on the mountain to deliver a new law, the
Sermon on the Mount. When Moses came down from the mountain,
his face was radiant from the encounter with God's glory; when Jesus
ascended a mountain (the Mount of Transfiguration, where he met
Moses and Elijah), his appearance was radiant, reflecting the glory
of God.

Returning to the Exodus account, during God's initial meeting
with Moses on Mount Sinai, Moses was told to prepare the people
for God's appearance on the mountaintop. They were to wash their
clothes and refrain from sexual intimacy. Moses was to erect a fence
before the mountain, telling the people not to touch the mountain.
Finally we read in Exodus:

> When morning dawned on the third day, there was thunder,
> lightning, and a thick cloud on the mountain, and a very loud
> blast of a horn. All the people in the camp shook with fear.
> Moses brought the people out of the camp to meet God, and

they took their place at the foot of the mountain. Mount Sinai was all in smoke because the LORD had come down on it with lightning. The smoke went up like the smoke of a hot furnace, while the whole mountain shook violently. The blasts of the horn grew louder and louder. Moses would speak, and God would answer him with thunder. The LORD came down on Mount Sinai to the top of the mountain. The LORD called Moses to come up to the top of the mountain, and Moses went up.

(Exodus 19:16-20)

The reader of Exodus is meant to feel the awe experienced by the Israelites in these encounters with God. The people were terrified. It was a dangerous thing to be in such proximity to the One by whose power the universe came into existence. I am reminded of the constant refrain in C. S. Lewis's novels about the land of Narnia regarding its king, the lion named Aslan, who represented Christ: "He is not a tame lion." Yahweh has compassion, mercy, and love for his people; nevertheless, his power and presence can't be contained in the tame versions of God that many of us believe in today. We're meant to take seriously the fear and awe that God inspired as he appeared at Sinai that day.

These powerful encounters in which God revealed himself to the Israelites on Mount Sinai were the reason that, centuries later, the prophet Elijah returned to this mountain to seek God. It is why pilgrims still come here to hike the mountain.

The Mountain of God

On the first day of our journey to the mountain, we encountered five or six buses of pilgrims at St. Catherine's, people from all over

On the road to Mount Sinai

the world. Most had only managed a few hours' sleep in their hotels before being awakened well before dawn to begin the climb up Mount Sinai. Some would hire camels for the journey up. Most would walk, staff in one hand, flashlight in the other. It takes two and a half to three hours to make it all the way to the top. Dress warm and bring gloves if you decide to make the trek.

I allowed our team to sleep in a bit, having pushed them hard the previous few days. We arrived on the mountain just before daybreak. The hike up was not terribly difficult, though sections would still leave an average person winded. At various points while hiking I would stop and open my Bible to the story of Moses' own journey up this mountain and the encounters he had there with God. I would pray, "Lord, please help me to meet you on this holy mountain."

The sun finally peeked over the top of the mountains as I prayed, and I felt its warmth on my face that cool morning. A feeling of peace washed over me, and a sense of God's presence and embrace. My encounter with God at Mount Sinai was more like that of Elijah, who heard God in a whisper, than that of Moses, who heard him in the thunder.[2]

At the top of Mount Sinai are two chapels. The first, a Greek Orthodox chapel usually closed to visitors, is the Church of the Holy Trinity. It was built in 1934 on the site of a much earlier church. The second is a mosque, also generally closed to the public. The tradition is that the original church on this site marked the place from which the stone came for the two tablets God used to etch the Ten Commandments. Such traditions are more about anchoring the story than testifying to a verifiable fact of history.

Exodus 20–24 describes a six-day period when God's glory covered the top of Mount Sinai, during which Moses received the Ten Commandments, as well as some other laws that constituted a basic legal code that would later be expanded. The Ten Commandments, also known as the Decalogue (the ten words), reflect God's basic ordering of Israelite society. Of the 613 commandments said to have been given by God to Moses, only these ten were etched in stone by the finger of God (Exodus 31:18). The stone tablets, representing the foundation of biblical ethics and the summation of the Law, were placed inside the Ark of the Covenant.

The Commandments

As I sat on the side of Mount Sinai, looking up at the sun rising over the summit, I took out my Bible, read the Ten Commandments, and reflected upon these pivotal commandments. It's worth noting that most of us don't like rules. We don't like people telling us "Thou shalt not" or even "Thou shalt." Some see the Ten Commandments in this way, as a kind of stifling set of commands. But I see them differently.

The commandments, then as now, function as theological statements and a vision for authentic human living. As theological statements, each tells us something about God and God's will for humanity. The statements offer a vision for how we live, love, and relate to one another. They help us know life's God-given boundaries. Ignore them and we cause or experience pain. Abide by them and we begin to live into God's will for humanity. They functioned in this way for the ancient Israelites, and they continue to function this way for us today.

Far from stifling us, the Ten Commandments are meant to keep us from harm and from succumbing to thoughts and behaviors that enslave. These particular commandments made it to the "top ten list" because they address some of the key temptations or tendencies with which human beings wrestle.

Let's take a look at the Ten Commandments and consider how they serve as God's rules of life. For those of you interested in reading more, you'll find several excellent books on related topics in "For Further Reading."

1. I am the LORD your God who brought you out of Egypt, out of the house of slavery. You must have no other gods before me.

(Exodus 20:2-3)

Some Christian traditions divide these first two lines into the first two commandments. Most Protestants consider Exodus 20:2-3 as a single commandment: "I am the LORD your God who brought you out of Egypt, out of the house of slavery. You must have no other gods before me." Under this scenario the second commandment is found in verses 4-6:

2. Do not make an idol for yourself—no form whatsoever—of anything in the sky above or on the earth below or in the waters under the earth. Do not bow down to them or worship them, because I, the LORD your God, am a passionate God. I punish children for their parents' sins even to the third and fourth generations of those who hate me. But I am loyal and gracious to the thousandth generation of those who love me and keep my commandments. (Exodus 20:4-6)

It appears that, during the hundreds of years when they lived in Egypt, the Israelites had adopted many religious beliefs of the Egyptians. But Yahweh had just made a mockery of the Egyptian gods by means of the plagues and had clearly defeated Pharaoh, considered by the Egyptians to be semidivine. Now, as God entered into a covenant with the Israelites, he made it clear that Israel was to have no other gods before him, nor were they to make graven images (carved idols or other representations) of deities in order to worship them or find security in them. It's as if God was saying, "I am *your* God, and I will not share your allegiance with another."

The Egyptians regularly made graven images of their gods. You can see these images covering the walls of Egypt's temples. Small statuettes of the deities were kept by people as expressions of the deities' presence, providing a sense of security. In tourist shops you can find modern versions of these idols: eight-inch cats, the warrior goddess Bastet, or similarly sized jackals carved of stone and representing Anubis, who weighed the hearts of the dead to determine if they would pass on to the afterlife.

God forbade the making of statuettes to represent him. He forbade creating images that would be worshiped. And he forbade the worship of any other gods.

St. Augustine captured the truth behind the first two commandments when he famously penned these words: "Thou hast made us for thyself, O Lord, and our heart is restless until it finds its rest in thee." When we put other things in place of God, something is amiss in our hearts.

These days we don't make little statuettes and call them gods. So how do these first two commandments speak to us today? If we recognize that a god is that which is of the highest importance in our lives—what we serve, what we desire above all else, what we turn to for security, what shapes our soul and identity, what drives us, gives us meaning, or is the center of our attention—then perhaps we might recognize our own tendencies toward idolatry.

What drives you? Status? Sex? Sports? Shopping? For some of us, our god is politics, and our political views overshadow our religious views.

What idols do you struggle with?

3. Do not use the LORD your God's name as if it were of no significance; the LORD won't forgive anyone who uses his name that way.

(Exodus 20:7)

The name of God is to be revered; it is holy. Some scholars look at this command and believe it forbids swearing oaths in God's name when one does not intend to keep the oath, or invoking God's name in support of something God would not favor. Many Jews will not say the personal name for God, *Yahweh*, for fear of inadvertently violating the commandment. Some will not even say or write the word *God*. Perhaps you have Jewish friends who write G_D to avoid the possibility of misusing even that word.

It's easy to think of the hellish things that have been done in the name of God: people who shout "God is great" before acts of terrorism or who invoke God's name to justify their bigotry or bullying. I think about a group of "Christians" from a church in Topeka, Kansas, who on several occasions stood across the street from the church I serve to hold up signs declaring that God hates gay and lesbian people.

Most of us are not in danger of grossly violating the commandment in this way, but we're still at risk of using God's name *as if it were of no significance.* We do so when we invoke God's name with certainty for positions we hold to be true but which may not in fact reflect God's views. This often happens in the realm of politics. After a recent election, I heard a national leader say that, with this election, "God has returned to Washington, D.C." Other Christians have proclaimed just the opposite. Both cannot be right, and it is likely that neither captures the truth about God's role in politics or God's presence in our nation's capital.

The spirit of the third commandment seems to exclude casual use of the word *God*. I often hear Christians using the word as an exclamation when they are upset, frustrated, or otherwise expressing their feelings. Each of these uses seems to constitute speaking God's name as though it were of no significance.

Do you ever use God's name as if it were of no significance? If you do, I invite you to be intentional in working to change that.

4. Remember the Sabbath day and treat it as holy. (Exodus 20:8)

Jonathan Sacks, formerly Chief Rabbi of the United Kingdom, writes, "When the Greeks and the Romans first encountered Jews, they could not understand Shabbat. They knew the concept of a holy day—every religion has such days. What they had never before encountered was a day made holy by rest, a day of being rather than doing."[3]

We keep the Sabbath by making space in our lives for worship, but we also keep it by refraining from work in order to rest and renew. This commandment is both a gift from God—a reminder of God's care for us—and an expression of our reverence for God. It is meant to be a part of the rhythm of our lives; even the animals are meant to have a day of rest. Sabbath reconnects us to God, honoring God, while at the same time renewing our own souls.

Most of us are too busy all the time. I know people who retire and say they are busier in retirement than when they were working. We take a vacation and come back worn out, needing a vacation from our vacation. We don't seem to know how to rest, recharge, and renew. I wonder if the fourth commandment may be even more essential today than it was in the time of Moses.

In addition to the toll our pace of life is taking on our health, well-being, and relationships with others, it also affects our faith and relationship with God. Worship attendance is waning across many different religious traditions. Frequency of attendance, even among committed Christians, is in decline. When asked why they are not in attendance more often, many note that they are "too busy," or they describe the host of activities that preclude their participating.

Our body, our mind, our spirit, our relationships are all built for Sabbath. We need rest, renewal, and worship. How are you doing in observing the rhythm of Sabbath—in honoring God through worship and in practicing rest and renewal? And on the Sabbath, are you intentional and committed about participating in a congregation where you can join with others to worship God—to keep the Sabbath holy by recognizing that it belongs to God?

5. *Honor your father and your mother. (Exodus 20:12)*

Beginning with the fifth commandment, the Ten Commandments turn from our relationship with God to our relationships with, responsibilities toward, and ethical treatment of others. The fifth commandment addresses our most foundational human relationship, the relationship with our parents.

In biblical times, the social contract involved parents taking care of their children, and then children, in turn, taking care of their aging parents. The contract changed in the last hundred years, owing to factors such as Social Security, retirement accounts, longer life expectancy, and better health care. But the needs of our parents are more than just physical or financial; seniors also need care and emotional support from their children and grandchildren.

The Apostle Paul wrote in Ephesians 6:2-3 that the fifth commandment is the only one that comes with a promise: "...*so that things will go well for you, and you will live for a long time in the land.*" Notice it doesn't say that by honoring your parents, their lives will be long; it says that by honoring them, *your* life will be long. I believe this is because we will have modeled for our children, and for other young people, the value and importance of caring for parents and others as they grow older. And it signifies the blessings of God that come as a result.

There are some for whom this commandment is particularly difficult. For those whose parents were abusive, unkind, or otherwise hurtful it is difficult to know how to "honor" a dishonorable parent without enabling or excusing unhealthy behavior. Sitting down with a pastor, counselor, or therapist can be helpful in discerning how to do this in a way that might bring healing to the child and repentance and redemption for the parent.

Are you treating your parents or grandparents in such a way that they know they have value and worth (the essential meaning of "honor" in Hebrew)? Is there more you can and should be doing for your own parents, or perhaps for older adults who don't have children of their own? If you have children, are you modeling this behavior for them?

6. Do not kill. (Exodus 20:13)

The sixth commandment reminds us that life belongs to God and is not ours to take. Keep in mind, however, that the Old Testament did make provision for the death penalty. It allowed for self-defense and for war. It recognized a distinction between accidental death—what we call manslaughter—and murder. So while killing in war was a necessary but tragic eventuality, and some would be put to death through the criminal justice system, broadly speaking the taking of life is not permitted, because it is not ours to take.

The commandment was largely about vengeance and retribution, though it also spoke for the value of life and against any kind of indiscriminate killing. Jesus took this commandment a step further in his Sermon on the Mount:

"You have heard that it was said to those who lived long ago, *Don't commit murder*, and all who commit murder will be in danger of judgment. But I say to you that everyone who is angry with their brother or sister will be in danger of judgment. If they say to their brother or sister, 'You idiot,' they will be in danger of being condemned by the governing council. And if they say, 'You fool,' they will be in danger of fiery hell."

(Matthew 5:21-22)

Once more Jesus made life a bit more difficult for his followers. I feel reasonably sure I will never kill another human being. But I've shouted, "You fool!" or its equivalent more than a few times. Jesus extended the commandment even further when he said, "Love your enemies and pray for those who persecute you" (Matthew 5:44 NRSV).

The sixth commandment—that God alone claims the right to end life—has far-reaching personal and ethical implications. It's clear, though, that in all cases our reasoning should in some way be affected by our understanding that, as stated in the sixth commandment, human life is sacred and is not ours to take.

In what way does the sixth commandment—either as conceived by Moses or reinterpreted by Jesus—speak to you?

7. Do not commit adultery. (Exodus 20:14)

Most human beings have an innate desire for both romantic love and sexual intimacy. The seventh commandment offers a vision of human love that involves a covenant to give one's romantic and sexual love exclusively to one's mate. We capture this vision in our marriage vows when we ask that the bride and the groom pledge "to have and to hold from this day forward, for better, for worse, for richer, for poorer, in sickness and in health, to love and to cherish, until we are parted by death."[4]

To some people, this idea of marriage and fidelity might seem antiquated. They may be surprised to learn, however, that some of our twentieth- and twenty-first-century sexual innovations are not really so innovative. Ancient societies, including the Egyptians and Israelites, had the same desires, tensions, and tendencies we see today. Pornography, infidelity, open marriage, polygamy, and more were present in those ancient societies. We even find these practices in Scripture: King Solomon had seven hundred wives and three hundred concubines.

In all these issues of sexuality, the seventh commandment serves as our guide. More helpful still were Jesus' words in the Sermon on the Mount, in which he reinterpreted this commandment: "You have heard that it was said, *Don't commit adultery*. But I say to you that every man who looks at a woman lustfully has already committed adultery in his heart" (Matthew 5:27-28).

Both the commandment and the words of Jesus affirm the concept of covenant loyalty and faithfulness within the bonds of marriage. The seventh commandment requires fidelity to the marriage vow. Jesus extended the concept to the thoughts of our heart.

The commandment is not intended to keep us from enjoying life; rather, it is meant to keep us from hurting ourselves and others by pursuing what is emotionally and spiritually damaging to us. Having this commandment helps us in difficult and tempting areas of life to know what is and isn't God's will.

Looking at your own life, what are the dangers of violating this commandment and the blessings of keeping it?

8. Do not steal. (Exodus 20:15)

This commandment seems pretty straightforward, right? Don't break into other people's homes and take things that don't belong to you. Most of us are not inclined to do that. But, like the other commandments, there is more here than meets the eye.

As I was writing this book, a major financial institution announced it had terminated thousands of employees because the employees, in order to meet sales goals and collect fees, had created fake bank and credit card accounts, or encouraged or pressured customers into creating such accounts. The *Wall Street Journal* called it the biggest scandal of the year.[5] This is just one example of a high-tech form of stealing.

If you've cheated on your taxes, misreported the value of a donation, filed a fraudulent insurance claim, sold a house or car without disclosing a known problem that would have reduced its value, then you have violated this commandment.

Years ago I heard the story of a man being considered for a promotion at work. A member of the Human Resources team was behind him in line at the cafeteria and watched as he picked up the various dishes that would comprise his lunch. Near the end of the line, the HR director noticed that the man slid a five-cent pat of butter under his napkin where it couldn't be seen as he approached the cash register. The HR director later called the man to her office to explain why he would not be getting the promotion: "I saw you hide that pat of butter under your napkin in the cafeteria line today.

I learned that your integrity had a pretty low price tag—just five cents."

What price does your integrity have?

9. Do not testify falsely against your neighbor. (Exodus 20:16)

The ninth commandment calls us to tell the truth about others. It specifically applies to testifying before a judge in a court case. The courts, and our broader human society, require trust. A false testimony could cost an individual his or her life or reputation or family. Society only works when we're honest and not deceitful about others.

Most of us would never falsely testify about someone in court. But how many times have we said something uncharitable about others at the water cooler at work? How many times have we shared our opinion about others as though it were fact? How many times have we tweeted information about others that was harmful and didn't reflect the truth? Today, thanks to social media, character assassination is easier than ever.

During a recent election campaign, news circulated that a pizza restaurant was a front for a child sex-trafficking operation that supposedly was connected to one of the candidates. The story was completely fabricated, but the restaurant owner began to receive death threats. One man read the story and, believing it to be true, showed up at the restaurant with guns drawn to rescue the children being trafficked.[6] Of course, there were no children being trafficked. It was just a pizza parlor, and the man was promptly arrested. In this case, the false testimony intended to impugn a candidate's character ended up nearly costing someone his life.

Do you ever assume the worst about someone, then share your assumptions? Have you passed on incendiary news from the Internet without verifying that it's true? Have you participated in gossip, backbiting, or speaking ill of others? If you have, then you have struggled with the ninth commandment.

10. You shall not covet. *(Exodus 20:17 NRSV)*

The tenth commandment shifts our focus from the actual deeds prohibited in earlier commandments, such as adultery or stealing, to the *desires* giving birth to those deeds.[7]

We desire what our neighbors have. Sometimes we call this "keeping up with the Joneses." The challenge today is that our entire economic system is built on cultivating discontent with what we have and convincing us to want what others have. Our economy is fueled by discontentment and desire.

Now, this type of desire has its upside: it means that merchants and manufacturers constantly work to improve their wares so that we'll want the newest, latest, greatest version. The problem comes when we begin to believe that our happiness and fulfillment can be found in having more stuff. Once again Jesus spoke of this commandment when he said, "Be on your guard against all kinds of greed; for one's life does not consist in the abundance of possessions" (Luke 12:15 NRSV).

Covetousness, greed, materialism—interestingly, they all go back to the first commandment. Who or what in our lives do we treat as god? Where do we find our meaning, our purpose, our end? What is the source of our deepest delight?

Jesus captured it well when he said, "Desire first and foremost God's kingdom and God's righteousness, and all these things will be given to you as well" (Matthew 6:33). The words of Isaiah also come to mind:

All of you who are thirsty, come to the water!
Whoever has no money, come, buy food and eat!
Without money, at no cost, buy wine and milk!
Why spend money for what isn't food,
    and your earnings for what doesn't satisfy?
                                              (Isaiah 55:1-2)

Do you ever struggle with covetousness?

This final commandment, along with all the others, was given not to deny us happiness but to free us from the things that enslave us and to give us life.

The Blood of the Covenant

After spending a day at Mount Sinai, I have a deep desire to return. I'd love to reserve several nights in a guest room at St. Catherine's Monastery, exploring the monastery by night, wandering on the mountainside by day, listening for the whisper of God. My first visit, though brief, was literally and spiritually a mountaintop experience.

There's so much more I'd like to reflect upon with you from the period of Moses' sojourn at Mount Sinai. These rich stories reveal God's character, raise serious questions, and speak to God's will. I'll leave them to you to discover.

Moses built an altar at the base of the mountain, where the people made sacrifices to God.

I want to end by noting that, for those of you who are Christians, as you read the stories you'll find again and again parallels to things written in the New Testament—the words of Jesus, the events of his life, the teachings from the Epistles. Allow me to point out one as I close this chapter.

After presenting the Ten Commandments in Exodus 20, Moses went back up the mountain and was given a set of case laws and expansions of the Ten Commandments. These are found in Exodus 20:20–23:33. Together with the Ten Commandments, they constitute the covenant God made with Israel and Israel with God. In Exodus 24, Moses built an altar at the base of the mountain, where the people made sacrifices to God. He took half the blood from the sacrifices and sprinkled it on the altar, then took the other half and sprinkled it on the people, saying, "This is the blood of the covenant that the LORD now makes with you on the basis of all these words" (Exodus 24:8).

Christians recognize these words, as Jesus alluded to them on the night of the Last Supper. Jesus said as he took the wine, "This is my blood of the covenant" (Matthew 26:28). He himself would be the sacrifice, the ensign, and the means of a new covenant between God and all humanity.

Following Moses' dramatic words and act at the altar, God told Moses to bring Aaron, his two sons, and Israel's seventy elders, and to meet him on the mountain for a covenant meal:

> Then Moses and Aaron, Nadab and Abihu, and seventy elders of Israel went up, and they saw Israel's God. Under God's feet there was what looked like a floor of lapis-lazuli tiles, dazzlingly pure like the sky. God didn't harm the Israelite leaders, though they looked at God, and they ate and drank.
>
> (Exodus 24:9-11)

God made a covenant with Israel, a covenant that included—as was ancient practice—the slaughter of an animal, the sprinkling of blood, and the sharing of a meal. This covenant ceremony and meal in Exodus 24 seem to be the backdrop for Jesus' words at the Last Supper and the Christian pattern of remembering and marking this covenant with bread and wine, a communing not only with fellow believers but with God. Each time believers share in this meal, they receive and renew Christ's covenant with them and they with him.

Exodus 24 ends with these words:

Then Moses went up the mountain, and the cloud covered the mountain. The LORD's glorious presence settled on Mount Sinai, and the cloud covered it for six days. On the seventh day the LORD called to Moses from the cloud. To the Israelites, the LORD's glorious presence looked like a blazing fire on top of the mountain. Moses entered the cloud and went up the mountain. Moses stayed on the mountain for forty days and forty nights (verses 15-18).

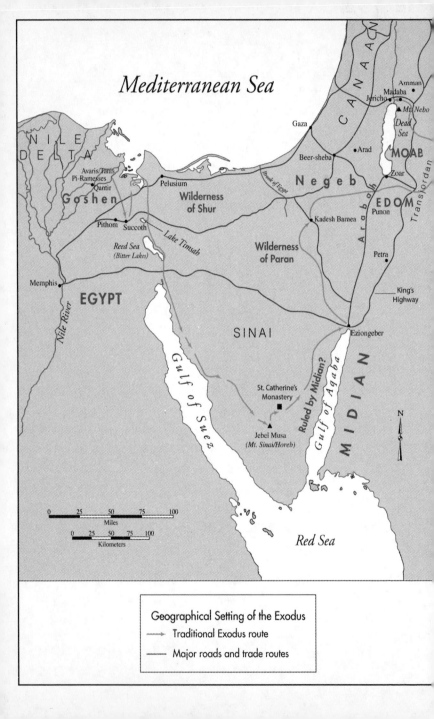

Mediterranean Sea

NILE DELTA

Avaris/Tanis
Pi-Ramesses
Qantir

Goshen

Pelusium

Wilderness
of Shur

Gaza

Amman
Madaba
Jericho
Mt. Nebo
Dead
Sea

MOAB

Beer-sheba

Arad

Negeb

Zoar

EDOM

Brook of Egypt

Kadesh Barnea

Punon

Translordan

Pithom

Succoth

Reed Sea
(Bitter Lakes)

Lake Timsah

Wilderness
of Paran

Petra

Arabah

Memphis

EGYPT

Nile River

Gulf of Suez

SINA I

King's
Highway

Eziongeber

Ruled by Midian?

St. Catherine's
Monastery

Gulf of Aqaba

MIDIAN

Jebel Musa
(Mt. Sinai/Horeb)

N

0   25   50   75   100
Miles

0   25   50   75   100
Kilometers

Red Sea

Geographical Setting of the Exodus

→ Traditional Exodus route

— Major roads and trade routes

5.

LESSONS FROM THE
WILDERNESS

Scripture tells us that from the day Moses freed the Israelites to the day he died at Mount Nebo, when the Israelites were about to enter the Promised Land, forty years passed, a period typically referred to as the Wilderness Wandering.

The wilderness was the vast Sinai Peninsula, where Israel would spend those forty years. The shortest path from Egypt to the Promised Land, with the smoothest road, was along the coast of the Mediterranean Sea, on an ancient trade route. The route was 130 miles long and easily could have been completed in a month. Why didn't the Israelites travel this route?

As we learned earlier, and as Exodus 13:17-18 explains, the trade route went through the land of the Philistines, who later became Israel's great enemy. "God thought, *If the people have to fight and face war, they will run back to Egypt.* So God led the people by the round-about way of the Reed Sea desert."[1] In addition, God had sworn to Moses that the people would worship at Mount Sinai, where God had first revealed himself to Moses and had called Moses to liberate the Israelite slaves.

As we trace the Israelites' forty-year journey through the Sinai, we'll touch on several highlights of Moses' leadership. We'll also devote a few pages to the construction of the Tent of Meeting. The writer of Exodus spends more time on instructions for building the Tent of Meeting and its furnishings than on the actual Exodus from Egypt, so we'll ponder the significance of this portable sanctuary.

Most importantly, we'll focus on three lessons that Moses, the Israelites, and we ourselves can learn from wandering in the wilderness.

Jethro's Advice to Moses

One day, as Moses and the Israelites were camped near Mount Sinai, Moses' father-in-law Jethro, Midian's priest, came to see him. Moses told Jethro the amazing things God had done to deliver the Israelites.

> Jethro said, "Bless the LORD who rescued you from the Egyptians' power and from Pharaoh's power, who rescued the people from Egypt's oppressive power. Now I know that the LORD is greater than all the gods."
>
> (Exodus 18:10-11)

In Exodus 18:13 we read, "The next day Moses sat as a judge for the people, while the people stood around Moses from morning until evening." Jethro, looking on, saw that it would be impossible for Moses to personally resolve every problem for all the people. It was an overwhelming task.

> Moses' father-in-law said to him, "What you are doing isn't good. You will end up totally wearing yourself out, both you and these people who are with you. The work is too difficult for you. You can't do it alone. Now listen to me and let me give you some advice."
>
> (Exodus 18:17-19)

Jethro was about to become one of history's first management consultants! He told Moses,

> "Look among all the people for capable persons who respect God. They should be trustworthy and not corrupt. Set these persons over the people…as judges for the people at all times. They should bring every major dispute to you, but they should decide all of the minor cases themselves.…They will share your load.…And all these people will be able to go back to their homes much happier."
>
> (Exodus 18:21-23)

What do management consultants call this? Delegating!

Moses made the mistake most leaders make from time to time. He felt as the leader that it was his job to do everything, particularly if he wanted it done right. But shared leadership and delegation are two fundamental principles of any successful leader. I remember when we began the Church of the Resurrection twenty-six years ago.

I personally called on every first-time visitor at home within twenty-four hours of their visit. I made every hospital visit. I attended every committee meeting. For every event and every program at the church, I felt I had to be there. I tried to keep my hands on everything. I was working seventy hours a week and felt like I was drowning.

Finally I spoke to a wise pastor, John Ed Mathison, who was serving one of the leading United Methodist churches in the country. He told me, in essence, what Jethro told Moses: "You've got to decide if this is your church or God's church. You've got to let go of the need to be at everything and do everything. You've got to turn that over to other people. Otherwise the church will never be anything more than it is today, and you'll be burned out before you're thirty." He was right, and I made a midcourse correction. I began to see that part of my job was to recruit, equip, and inspire others to do ministry. That made all the difference.

Go back and read Exodus 18, the entire chapter. I think you'll find four steps that Jethro the consultant gave Moses:

1. Choose the right people—capable, reverent, and trustworthy.
2. Train the people well.
3. Empower and authorize them in front of the people they will be leading.
4. Make clear what needs approval and what they can decide on their own.

It always seems easier, at first, to do everything yourself. But as the work expands, whether you are in leadership in a church or in the corporate world, you will be more effective and more likely to be fruitful if you raise up, train, and share leadership. Sometimes churches think they hire the pastor to do the work of ministry, but the Apostle Paul says the job of the pastor is to prepare God's people to do the work. (The pastor shares in this work and models how it is done, but equally as important is sharing the leadership and raising others up to serve.)

How are you doing at sharing leadership?

Building the Tent of Meeting

Shortly after his meeting with Jethro, Moses led the people to camp at the base of Mount Sinai, where they would remain for the next eleven months. In the previous chapter we considered Moses' encounter with God at Mount Sinai, the giving of the Ten Commandments, the nucleus of the Law, and the covenant God made with the Israelites there. Following these momentous events, we read:

> The LORD said to Moses: Tell the Israelites to collect gift
> offerings for me. Receive my gift offerings from everyone
> who freely wants to give.... They should make me a sanctuary
> so I can be present among them. You should follow the
> blueprints that I will show you for the dwelling and for all its
> equipment.
>
> (Exodus 25:1-2, 8-9)

The next seven chapters of Exodus give a detailed description of the sanctuary God wanted built, the Tent of Meeting. Following that, Exodus 35–39 describes what architects today call FF&E—the furniture, fixtures, and equipment needed in the sanctuary. More space in the Book of Exodus is devoted to God's instructions for

The Tent of Meeting

building the Tent of Meeting than to the story of the plagues and the Exodus combined. Clearly this sanctuary was important to God.

As we saw history's first management consultant in Exodus 18, in Exodus 25 we find history's first capital campaign, or at least the first one recorded in the Bible. God told Moses to cast a vision to the Israelites for the sanctuary, a portable tent that would be God's dwelling place among the people during their travels. The people, at this point living in the wilderness in their own tents, gave freely of what they had. The campaign was so successful that in Exodus 36 we read:

> The skilled workers building the sanctuary left their work that they were doing one by one to come and say to Moses, "The people are contributing way too much material for doing the work that the LORD has commanded us to do."

> So Moses issued a command that was proclaimed throughout the camp: "Every man and woman should stop making gift offerings for the sanctuary project." So the people stopped bringing anything more because what they had already brought was more than enough to do all the work.
>
> (Exodus 36:4-7)

By the way, this is every pastor's dream of a capital campaign!

The sanctuary, Exodus tells us, was a tent that would be pitched in the center of the Israelite camp, with the tents of the people of Israel on all four sides. It was to be a visible symbol of God's presence in the midst of the people. Interestingly, the tent seems to have been patterned after the tent of Pharaoh Ramesses II, which was used in the Battle of Kadesh in Syria as Ramesses was attacking the Hittites, a battle that took place in 1274 B.C. just a few years before the Exodus.

The Tent of Meeting may have been patterned after the tent of Pharaoah Ramesses II, where the pharaoh made offerings to the Egyptian god Amun-Ra.

Today the tent of Ramesses, a portable palace that was erected when Pharaoh was leading the Egyptians into battle, can be seen in bas reliefs depicting scenes from the battle.

Both Pharaoh's tent and God's Tent of Meeting had an open-air outer courtyard that was twice as long as it was wide. Each had an inner tent three times longer than it was wide, and the inner tent was divided into two rooms, one larger and one smaller. The smallest of the rooms was, in both cases, a throne room. Pharaoh's throne was depicted as having two winged creatures on each side, protecting the Pharaoh. In the case of God's Tent of Meeting, an area called the Most Holy Place, or the Holy of Holies, also had a throne—the Ark of the Covenant—that had two winged cherubim on each end.

The connection between king and god in Egypt was clear. For Israel, God was her King. The sanctuary Moses was asked to build was both temple and palace.

The Tent of Meeting, sometimes called the Tabernacle, was a portable structure intended to be a visible symbol of the invisible God's presence in the midst of his people wherever they camped. Erected at the center of the camp, it was not only the largest structure in the camp but also the most beautiful. God gave directions for the colors of yarn used to weave the tent, and the pattern included winged cherubim. The items in the Tent of Meeting were masterfully carved and covered in gold. The throne of God—the Ark of the Covenant—was particularly important. The top, made of pure gold with the two winged cherubim on each end, is variously called the "cover" or the "mercy seat," depending upon the translation of the Bible one is reading.[2] Here the high priest would come once a year to offer the blood of a bull to make atonement for the sins of the people.[3]

The lid of the Ark sat atop a gold-covered box, inside of which were the stone tablets containing the Ten Commandments. When the Israelites were traveling, the Ark was carried ahead of the people as a reminder that God went ahead of them, leading them on their way.

Exodus ends with the building of the Tent of Meeting and these words:

> When Moses had finished all the work, the cloud covered
> the meeting tent and the LORD's glorious presence filled the
> dwelling. Moses couldn't enter the meeting tent because the
> cloud had settled on it, and the LORD's glorious presence
> filled the dwelling. Whenever the cloud rose from the

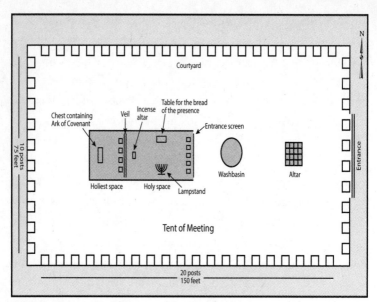

Diagram showing possible layout of the Tent of Meeting

dwelling, the Israelites would set out on their journeys. But if the cloud didn't rise, then they didn't set out until the day it rose. The LORD's cloud stayed over the dwelling during the day, with lightning in it at night, clearly visible to the whole household of Israel at every stage of their journey.

(Exodus 40:33-38)

As I write this book, I've been thinking a lot about sacred architecture and spaces where people gather to meet God. The church I pastor has been building its permanent sanctuary after twenty-six years of worshiping in a funeral home, an elementary school gym, a small chapel, our student center, and our fellowship hall. Perhaps you would indulge me, as we think of the Tent of Meeting, to offer a few reflections about sacred spaces—places devoted to the worship of God.

As we've seen, the Tent of Meeting or Tabernacle was more than a building; it was a visible reminder of God's presence. Its royal character signified that God, not Moses or Pharaoh, was Israel's King. It was the place where people expressed penance, thanksgiving, or petition through the offerings they brought to the priests who served there. It would serve this function for nearly three hundred years until King David made plans to replace it with a temple built atop Mount Moriah in Jerusalem. This permanent Temple would be seen as God's earthly dwelling place. David's son Solomon would construct the Temple, the tallest and most magnificent structure in Jerusalem.

Solomon's Temple would stand for nearly four hundred years before being destroyed by the Babylonians in 586 B.C. It was rebuilt, though not to its previous glory, by Zerubbabel in 516 B.C. and stood for nearly five hundred years before being extensively remodeled (in essence, rebuilt) by King Herod beginning in 19 B.C. First-century Jewish historian Josephus records that there were ten thousand construction workers who helped to remodel the Temple. The foundation walls for the remodeled Temple are still visible in Jerusalem. Jews still come and pray before the western foundation wall, believing that the Temple—even just its remaining foundation walls—is a "thin space" where heaven and earth meet.

There was a time when the most beautiful and architecturally meaningful buildings in the world were churches and other religious structures. These were designed, like the Temple and the Tent of Meeting, to be visible reminders of God and, through their design and materials, to draw people to God and usher them into his presence. That practice, with a few notable exceptions, largely changed in the second half of the twentieth century. Today, meaningful and inspiring architecture seems primarily the domain of performing arts centers, museums, and the occasional office building.

Among the challenges for most churches today is cost. Pastors and building committees often find themselves in a position where they need to build as much space as possible for as little money as possible. Though sacred architecture doesn't have to be expensive, it will never be as cheap as a sanctuary that doubles as an auditorium or gymnasium. Add to the issue of cost the fact that in seminary, little or no time is devoted to the importance of sacred art and architecture as it relates to the worship experience. Perhaps as a result, many pastors have come to believe that art and architecture don't matter to the congregation, to the community, to the individual worshiper, or to God. Yet recent studies among millennials have found that, given the choice between an auditorium or a place of worship that "feels like a church," most would choose the latter.

At the Church of the Resurrection, several years before we broke ground on our sanctuary, we formed a team to study what the Bible says about sacred buildings—specifically about the Tent of Meeting and the Temple. We looked at Exodus 25–40, 1 Chronicles 22, and 1 Kings 5 to see what they might teach us about how God viewed places dedicated to him and representing him. We also looked to see what Jesus had to say about the Temple (a building that Jesus, both as a boy and later in his public ministry, called "my Father's house"). We visited churches of various types and discussed how the architecture informed and shaped the experience of those who gathered within.

But it was in reading Exodus that we came to believe that architecture matters to God.

Having said that, the Tent of Meeting was still a tent, which shows that any building might have elements that can foster a sense of sacredness for worshipers, even if its architecture is quite simple. At the Tent of Meeting there was the smell of incense. The altar, the candelabra, and the Ark of the Covenant fostered a sense of reverence. The colors and images in the tapestries all added to the sense that this was a holy place where God might be encountered.

We sense God's presence on mountaintops as Moses did at Mount Sinai. We often feel God's spirit at the ocean. We sense the greatness of God "when through the woods and forest glades" we wander. But are there churches where you have felt particularly close to God?[4] What was it that contributed to that feeling?

By the way, notice the reason God told Moses to build the tent: "They should make me a sanctuary so I can be present among them" (Exodus 25:8). Other translations say "so that I can dwell with them." Did God need a tent to be with the people and dwell with them? Of course not. So, who was that tent really for? It was for the people, so that every time they saw it, every time the Ark of the Covenant went out ahead of them, they would remember and know what was already true: that God was in their midst; God was with them.

When you drive past a church or synagogue, remember that for the congregations and communities that meet there, these buildings are like the Tent of Meeting—places where people go to meet God and find grace, hope, and love. These places are visible reminders of what is true but which we do not see: God is in our midst. What would happen if each time you drove past a religious building, you took a moment to pray and remember that God is with you?

The Sinai Wilderness

Once the Israelites completed God's Tabernacle, it was time for them to leave Mount Sinai and continue their journey toward the Promised Land. The Israelites would spend forty years in the wilderness of the Sinai Peninsula. When we traveled through that land, it was difficult for us to imagine how they could have survived. As we'll see in a moment, they themselves were regularly afraid they would not survive, and they were often none too happy that Moses had brought them to such a harsh and difficult land.

Before leaving for Egypt, James Ridgeway of Educational Opportunities Tours, a Christian travel service, had told me that places in the Sinai look like Mars. Comparing some of the photos taken by NASA's Mars rovers with the terrain we saw in the Sinai, I can tell you they do look surprisingly similar.

The Sinai Peninsula's topography begins with a wide plain to the north that runs along the Mediterranean Sea. The elevation rises slowly from sea level at the coast to one thousand feet above sea level sixty miles south of the sea. Another sixty miles south through the heart of the country, the altitude doubles to two thousand feet, a gentle climb to the limestone plateau that covers much of the middle of the Sinai. But from this point on, the grade increases rapidly as you enter mountains that are five thousand feet high. A few miles farther and the peaks rise over eight thousand feet above sea level, before beginning to decline rapidly as you reach the Red Sea at Sinai's tip.

Though we spent just a day exploring the landscape, in 1869 English explorer E. H. Palmer spent eleven months there, traversing

the Sinai peninsula on foot with a small expedition and local Bedouin guides. He wrote a fascinating book about the Sinai entitled *The Desert of the Exodus: Journeys on Foot in the Wilderness of the Forty Years' Wanderings.*[5] One of Palmer's traveling companions was his brother, Captain H. S. Palmer, who wrote of the Sinai, "It is a desert, certainly, in the fullest sense of the word, but a desert of rock, gravel, and boulder, of gaunt peaks, dreary ridges and arid valleys and plateaux, the whole forming a scene of stern desolation which fully merits its description as the 'great and terrible wilderness.'"[6]

When we speak of the forty-year "wilderness wandering" of the Israelites, the phrase is a bit of misnomer. The Israelites, after leaving Egypt, traveled for three months to Mount Sinai and remained there eleven months. (By way of reminder, everything from Exodus 19 to Numbers 10:10 is set during the eleven months at Mount Sinai.) Then the Israelites left Mount Sinai and made their way to a place called Kadesh or Kadesh Barnea, 155 miles north as the crow flies, assuming that the traditional location for Kadesh Barnea is correct.[7] The traditional location is shown on the map at the beginning of the chapter.

Depending upon the precise route the Israelites took from Mount Sinai to Kadesh Barnea, it would have taken less than a month to travel there. Following their arrival, the Israelites spent most of the next thirty-eight years camped at or near Kadesh Barnea. This means that of the forty years the Israelites spent in the wilderness, less than six months was spent "wandering." They spent eleven months at Mount Sinai and thirty-eight years at Kadesh Barnea, before moving on to Mount Nebo, a journey we will be discussing in the final chapter.[8]

Grumbling in the Wilderness

One of the major themes running through Exodus and the Book of Numbers is the criticizing and complaining of the Israelites. They grumbled against Moses and at times against God. There are ten such passages found in Exodus and Numbers. Most of the complaints had to do with food, drink, and living conditions in the Sinai wilderness, which was understandable. They had been slaves, but in a part of Egypt called Goshen, where there was plenty to eat, the land was verdant, and water plentiful. As we drove through the vast barren Sinai, through sand dunes, granite mountains with virtually nothing growing on them, and only the occasional oasis easily identified by palm trees, I found myself thinking, "No wonder they were complaining all the time!"

> The whole Israelite community complained against Moses
> and Aaron in the desert. The Israelites said to them, "Oh,
> how we wish that the LORD had just put us to death while we
> were still in the land of Egypt. There we could sit by the pots
> cooking meat and eat our fill of bread. Instead, you've brought
> us out into this desert to starve this whole assembly to death."
> (Exodus 16:2-3)

Bear in mind that this was just a few days after they had escaped Egypt! The Israelites didn't know it yet, but they had decades ahead of them in that wilderness.

But God heard their complaints and provided them with a flaky substance left on the ground with the morning dew and which they used like flour to make bread and cakes to eat. The Israelites gathered this substance every morning—just enough for the day so that they had to trust God the next day to provide once again. (This is what Jesus is alluding to when, in the Lord's Prayer, he invites us to pray, "Give us this day our daily bread." It's a prayer asking "just enough" for the day.) The Israelites called the substance *manna*, from a Hebrew word that means something like "What's that?!" They would then prepare it as described in Numbers 11:7-8.

> The manna was like coriander seed and its color was like resin.
> The people would roam around and collect it and grind it
> with millstones or pound it in a mortar. Then they would boil
> it in pots and make it into cakes. It tasted like cakes baked in
> olive oil.

Manna doesn't sound so bad for a day or two. But picking up this crust from the ground each day, grinding it to make bread, and eating the same thing over and over again might result in some complaining at my house. In Numbers 11:4-6 we read,

> The Israelites cried again and said, "Who will give us meat
> to eat? We remember the fish we ate in Egypt for free, the
> cucumbers, the melons, the leeks, the onions, and the garlic.
> Now our lives are wasting away. There is nothing but manna
> in front of us."

In response, though a bit peeved at their ingratitude, God sent a strong wind that blew in flocks of quail—millions of them. While we were in the wilderness we saw small flocks of birds in various places, reminding us of this story. Quail do migrate through the Sinai each year.

Once the people had had their fill of quail, they complained again, not just about the food and lack of water but about Moses' leadership for bringing them to the Sinai at all. Eventually they even began to complain about his wife, Zipporah. Some wanted to "fire" Moses and Aaron and choose new leaders. On several occasions they spoke of returning to Egypt.

When I read this story, I think about school teachers who have told me they feel like quitting after receiving notes and comments from parents complaining about their work. I think about one mother in our congregation who came to see me some years ago. She was so frustrated by her husband and children that she'd left them a note saying, "I'm running away and I'm not coming back." Her bags were packed; she was serious.

Everyone is criticized from time to time. Recently I was reading about presidential approval ratings in the twentieth century. Do you know who in that century was the most popular president? The figures vary depending upon the pollster, but according to one of the Gallup polls it was John Kennedy, with a 74 percent approval rating. He was followed by Ronald Reagan with 61 percent. Bill Clinton's approval rating was 55 percent. But think about it: that means that even for the presidents with the highest approval ratings, 26 percent, 39 percent, and 45 percent of the population, respectively, disapproved of the job they were doing![9]

One of my favorite stories of how leaders will be criticized is about two men named Doane Robinson and Gutzon Borglum, who had the crazy idea of sculpting the busts of four presidents out of a mountainside in South Dakota. People thought it was the worst idea they'd ever heard of. Why would anyone destroy a mountain like that? Why would anyone pick *those* four presidents? What a ridiculous expenditure of money when there were so many hungry people in the world. Newspapers, conservationists, preachers, and politicians all jumped on the bandwagon of criticism. And just as the project was getting started, the Great Depression struck. Today, though, no one criticizes Mount Rushmore. It is a national monument visited by over two million people annually,[10] and the one-million-dollar cost adds over $200 million a year to the local economy.[11]

I wonder if anyone has ever criticized you? How did it feel? If you are in a position of leadership, have people ever second-guessed your actions? Have you ever been fired? When you feel discouraged, remember Moses' story. He was one of the greatest leaders in all the Bible, and yet the Israelites wanted to fire him! As with many of us, the Israelites were shortsighted; they were sick of eating manna and quail, and they were willing to go back to Egypt as slaves if they could only have leeks and cucumbers.

I love Moses' response to these complaints. It expresses the way every leader feels from time to time.

> Moses said to the LORD, "Why have you treated your servant so badly? And why haven't I found favor in your eyes, for you have placed the burden of all these people on me? . . . I can't bear this people on my own. They're too heavy for me. If you're going to treat me like this, please kill me."
>
> (Numbers 11:11, 14-15)

A bit melodramatic, but you get the picture. We all feel like quitting sometimes in the face of criticism and complaining. But God didn't kill Moses, and he didn't let him quit. Instead God continued to call him, encourage him, and use him to lead the people.

Leadership is sometimes hard. Sometimes leaders feel like giving up. But the leaders who have an enduring impact *don't* give up. They listen to and learn from their critics, but they also keep marching forward toward their visions of the Promised Land.

Paralyzed by Fear Just Miles from the Promised Land

By Numbers 13, the Israelites had been free from slavery for two years. They were in the Wilderness of Paran, setting up camp at Kadesh Barnea. This was exciting—they were just a few miles from the Promised Land! After two long and arduous years, they were about to inherit the land that flowed with milk and honey, which Moses had described so many times.

At that point God commanded Moses, "Send out men to explore the land of Canaan, which I'm giving to the Israelites. Send one man from each ancestral tribe, each a chief among them" (Numbers 13:2).

The scouts spent the next forty days exploring the Promised Land. Here was the scouts' report when they returned: "We entered the land to which you sent us. It's actually full of milk and honey, and this is its fruit. There are, however, powerful people who live in the land. The cities have huge fortifications" (13:27-28).

Upon hearing this report, the people of Israel became anxious, but Caleb, one of the scouts, spoke up:

> "We must go up and take possession of it, because we are more than able to do it."

> But the men who went up with him said, "We can't go up against the people because they are stronger than we....All the people we saw in it are huge men....We saw ourselves as grasshoppers, and that's how we appeared to them."
> (Number 13:30-33)

Kadesh Barnea (the Wilderness of Paran)

Notice how the Israelites responded: they became paralyzed by fear.

> The entire community raised their voice and the people wept that night. All the Israelites criticized Moses and Aaron. The entire community said to them, "If only we had died in the land of Egypt or if only we had died in this desert! Why is the LORD bringing us to this land to fall by the sword? Our wives and our children will be taken by force. Wouldn't it be better for us to return to Egypt?" So they said to each other, "Let's pick a leader and let's go back to Egypt."
>
> (Numbers 14:1-4)

This was the tenth incident of the people complaining against Moses and, by implication, against God. The people even planned to stone Moses and Aaron! (14:10). Their attitude roused God's anger. After all God had done for them, the people still didn't trust God! And so God announced to Moses,

> None of the people who have seen my glory and the signs that I did in Egypt and in the wilderness, and yet have tested me these ten times and have not obeyed my voice, shall see the land that I swore to give to their ancestors; none of those who despised me shall see it.
>
> (Numbers 14:22-23 NRSV)

As a result of God's pronouncement, no one twenty years of age and older who had cried out against God and against Moses would be allowed to enter the Promised Land. Only Joshua and Caleb would go, because they had encouraged the people to enter the land and take it. This is the reason the Israelites spent the next thirty-eight years in the desert: they had allowed fear to stop them just miles from the Promised Land.

At times all of us wrestle with fear—of failure, of success, of others, of being poor, of growing old, and a thousand other fears. And our fear, when we give in to it, keeps *us* living in the wilderness, just a few miles outside the Promised Land.

It's not that there aren't legitimate things to fear. The people in the new land were strong and the cities were fortified, as the scouts had reported. But God was with the Israelites. And the God who parted the Reed Sea and raised Jesus Christ from the dead is also with us! That means that no matter how tall the giants may be, if God is with us we can move forward, and somehow, some way, he will lead us to the "Promised Land."

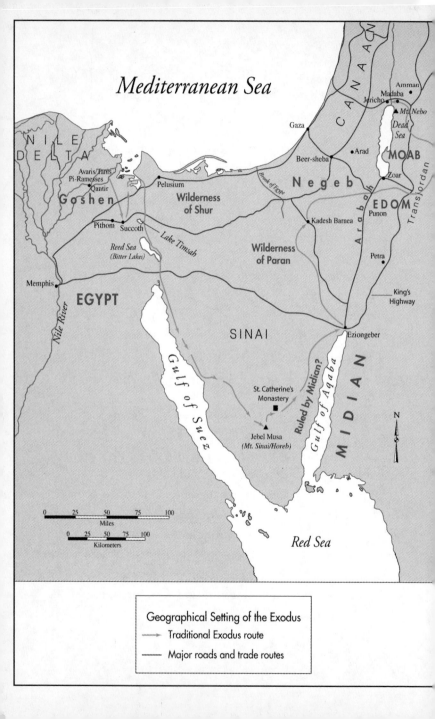

Geographical Setting of the Exodus

Traditional Exodus route

Major roads and trade routes

6.

DON'T FORGET...PASS IT ON

Deuteronomy is set in the final days of Moses' life. He had led the Israelites to the Jordan River, just east of the Promised Land. God told Moses that he would not actually enter the land with them; shortly he would ascend Mount Nebo, and there he would die. The book is composed of Moses' farewell discourses—his final words to the Israelites.

It is clear in reading Deuteronomy that Moses was worried that following his death, the people might forget who they were, *whose* they were, and why God had brought them to this land. In his final messages, Moses summarizes the journey they've been on together. He recites the most important parts of the Law. He reminds the

Israelites of their calling and mission as God's people. And he urges them to pass on their faith to their children. With this in mind, let's explore the final days of Moses' life and his parting words found in Deuteronomy.

The Journey to the Plains of Moab

In the last chapter we left the Israelites camped at Kadesh Barnea, paralyzed by fear a few miles from the Promised Land. When they refused to trust God to deliver the land into their hands, God decreed that the people would remain in the wilderness for forty years, until the generation that doubted God was gone. Only Joshua and Caleb from among that generation would enter the Land of Canaan. The remaining thirty-eight years (they had already been in the Sinai for two years) are only briefly recounted in the Book of Numbers. By Numbers 20, the thirty-eight years had passed. Moses was 120 years old, and the time had come for him to lead the Israelites from Kadesh Barnea to the Promised Land.

Rather than traveling due north just a few miles and entering Canaan from the south, Moses led the Israelites east for sixty-five miles, traveling the Reed Sea road to where it met the King's Highway, a major trade route east of the Jordan River. He planned for the Israelites to cross the shallow waters of the Jordan just north of the Dead Sea, near Jericho. Numbers 20–36 recounts this journey, including the death of Miriam and Aaron, Moses' sister and brother. These chapters include battles with the small kingdoms of Arad, Sihon, and Og, along with the slaughter of the Midianites, which began the violence that would continue into the Book of Joshua. This bloodshed raises serious ethical questions for most readers, questions that are beyond the scope of this book but which I discuss elsewhere.[1]

The Book of Numbers ends with Moses and the Israelites camped "in the plains of Moab by the Jordan across from Jericho" (Numbers 36:13). That is where Deuteronomy begins.

Exploring Jordan

The Israelites marched from the north-central Sinai to Jordan; we took a plane from Cairo to Jordan's capital city, Amman (which draws its name from the ancient Ammonites mentioned in the Bible). Our driver and guide met us at the airport and took us to our hotel overlooking the Dead Sea on the Jordanian side of the sea.

The Dead Sea is the lowest body of water on earth. Its water is more than eight times the salinity of the ocean, which leads to great buoyancy—you can easily float on it. From our hotel at the Dead Sea we would explore the areas where the Israelites camped and where Moses gave his final address, and we would climb Mount Nebo, where Moses died.

As we've learned before, modern roadways follow the ancient roads, and today Highway 15 and Highway 35 in Jordan are built near and in some places atop the ancient routes, which are still referred to as the King's Highway. Sections of a Roman road may be seen at various archaeological sites nearby.

As the highway makes its way to the plains of Moab, it passes some remarkable terrain. The Israelites would have skirted the edge of Wadi Mujib, known as the Grand Canyon of Jordan. They would have wound their way back and forth on the switchbacks that cross

Wadi Mujib, known as the Grand Canyon of Jordan

the beautiful Moab foothills and mountains, which are particularly remarkable at sunset as they glow in pink, orange, and red hues. Yet I suspect the Israelites, as they followed Moses, were not marveling at the rugged beauty of these lands; rather, I imagine them saying to Moses what my children used to say when we took them on road trips: "When are we going to be there?"

One of the towns the Israelites would have passed, mentioned in Numbers 21:30 as "Medeba," is the still-vibrant village of Madaba. The town straddled the King's Highway in ancient times and today is home to about sixty thousand people. Madaba is known today for the mosaic tile floor in the Church of St. George. The floor dates back to the A.D. 500s and is a detailed map of the biblical sites of the Holy Lands, including the most detailed picture scholars have of the

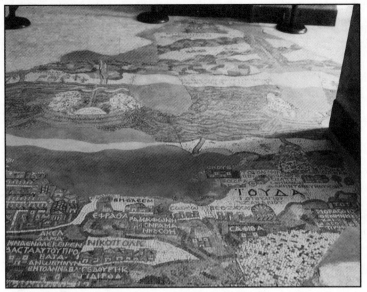

Madaba Map, showing biblical sites of the Holy Lands in the A.D. 500s

layout of sixth-century Jerusalem. Called today the Madaba Map, it was constructed using over two million ceramic tiles. The floor had remained hidden for centuries and was only rediscovered in 1896.

Following our exploration of Madaba, we made our way to the hillsides through which the Israelites would have passed before arriving at the plains of Moab. During the month of February, when we made our trip, the hills were green with vegetation, a stark contrast to the wilderness the Israelites would have just passed through. We saw sheep grazing, and groves of olive trees grew along with gardens in the valleys. It was easy to imagine the Israelites feeling hopeful as they passed through this land. On one of the hillsides, just above the plains of Moab, I stopped to imagine Moses addressing the Israelites one last time.

The Most Popular Book in the Torah

As Moses stood before the Israelites, he knew this would be the last time he would address them. They would enter the Promised Land without him. It had been eighty years since he had stood by and watched the Israelite slaves being worked to death by their Egyptian masters—eighty years since he had killed the Egyptian slavedriver, left his life as prince in Egypt, and fled to the Sinai. It had been forty years since he had heard the voice of God calling him from a burning bush, compelling him to return to Egypt to lead the Israelites to freedom. Moses stood there remembering his great confrontation with Pharaoh and the plagues and the day the Israelites passed through the Sea of Reeds with Pharaoh's army in pursuit.

Most of the people who stood before him that day had not even been born when God's glorious presence descended upon Mount Sinai with smoke and lightning. They had never seen the stone tablets with the Ten Commandments that Moses had sealed inside the Ark of the Covenant forty years earlier.

This was a new generation of people who hadn't known what it was to be a slave in Egypt and whose knowledge of their deliverance had come only from the stories their parents or grandparents had told them. The text of Deuteronomy tells us that Moses' heart was heavy that day, not because his death was imminent but because he feared that the Israelites would enter the land, become prosperous, and forget what God had done for them. He worried that they would slowly drift away from God and that the mission for which God had delivered them—to be a kingdom of priests making God known to the world—would be all but forgotten.

Deuteronomy means "second law," but it is not a second law; rather, it is a recitation and summation of Israel's story and God's covenant with her. It was written in the form of treaties that were common in the ancient Near East, called vassal treaties or suzerainty treaties.[2] Rising above this form, Moses' farewell speech is remarkably timeless. It was intended not merely for those in the past; instead, it is addressed to every generation who continue to read it and claim the Exodus story as their own. In it, they will hear the call not to forget who they are and whose they are, and they will learn the importance of passing on their faith to future generations. As such, it speaks as powerfully today as it did when it was first written.[3]

Because Deuteronomy is written as a series of sermons or addresses, summing up Israel's story and God's law, it flows more smoothly, is easier to follow, and is much shorter than the combined accounts of Exodus, Leviticus, and Numbers. For this reason, Deuteronomy became one of the most loved and frequently read books of the Hebrew Bible. Thirty copies of Deuteronomy were found among the Dead Sea Scrolls, making it the second most common book of the Hebrew Bible found there after the Book of Psalms (thirty-six copies of the Psalms were found).[4] Likewise, in the Gospels, Jesus quotes Deuteronomy more often than any other text in his Bible except for the Psalms. This preference is clearly seen in the story of Jesus' temptations, when to each temptation Jesus responds with a verse from Deuteronomy.

Passing on the Faith

If there is one theme that stands above the rest in the farewell discourses of Moses that make up the Book of Deuteronomy, it would be Moses' concern that the Israelites pass on the faith to their children. Thirty-eight verses in Deuteronomy mention children. Many passages are similar to these:

> These words that I am commanding you today must always be on your minds. Recite them to your children. Talk about them when you are sitting around your house and when you are out and about, when you are lying down and when you are getting up.
>
> (Deuteronomy 6:6-7)

Why was this admonition important to Moses? So that "you and your children and your children's children may fear the LORD your God all the days of your life" (6:2 NRSV). Note this same emphasis a few verses later:

> When your children ask you in time to come, "What is the meaning of the decrees and the statutes and the ordinances that the LORD our God has commanded you?" then you shall say to your children, "We were Pharaoh's slaves in Egypt, but the LORD brought us out of Egypt with a mighty hand. The LORD displayed before our eyes great and awesome signs and wonders against Egypt, against Pharaoh and all his household. He brought us out from there in order to bring us in, to give us the land that he promised on oath to our ancestors. Then the LORD commanded us to observe all these statutes, to fear the LORD our God, for our lasting good, so as to keep us alive, as is now the case. If we diligently observe this entire commandment before the LORD our God, as he has commanded us, we will be in the right."
>
> (Deuteronomy 6:20-25)

There is an urgency to Moses' words. He knew that Israel's faith, the faith he had devoted himself to, would be "never more than one generation away from extinction."[5]

Moses' concern is part of what makes Deuteronomy so timeless. Every generation faces this same challenge. For example, there has been a significant focus in the past few years on the declining religious affiliation among millennials and the overall decline in worship attendance among people of all ages. Some suggest, however, that the sky is not falling. Haydn Shaw, in his book *Generational IQ*, reminds us that young adults have always dropped out of church in their late teens and returned when they start having children. He notes that millennials are waiting much longer to marry and have children than young people did twenty years ago, which means they are also waiting longer to come back to church.[6] I think he's right, but that fact alone does not completely explain the decline in religious affiliation and participation that we're seeing today.

I believe that Moses' words in Deuteronomy continue to be the key to the future of faith. In teaching faith to our children, we don't want to be guilty of "cramming it down their throats." But I fear that, for most of us, that's not the problem. We may take our kids to church and even Sunday school, but we sometimes fail to have meaningful, authentic conversations with them concerning what *we* really believe about God, how we've seen God work in our lives, and what we have experienced of God in prayer and worship—conversations that are not forced but come out of our daily attempts to walk with God.

As our children grow up, particularly if they move away from God and the church for a period of time, it becomes harder to have such conversations. During these seasons with my own kids, after they had graduated from high school and had gone away to college, I found it easier to write letters to them conveying my love to them, in which perhaps one paragraph out of seven or eight might be about faith. As a family we continued to pray at mealtime when the girls came home to visit, even if one or the other of them did not bow their heads. I tried to stop preaching and pushing, while at the same time praying and striving to demonstrate something real in my faith that might one day speak to them.

Now that I'm a grandfather to a three-year-old granddaughter, I'm wondering if grandparents may be an important key to passing on the faith to future generations. My grandmother Sarah had the greatest impact on my faith when I was a boy. A devout Roman Catholic, she took me to church. Since I was seldom with her on Sunday, she took me to Bingo with the nuns on Friday or to light a candle and walk through the church on a weekday. She taught me to pray the Rosary and was intentional about sharing her faith. It was in reading a Bible she had given our family that I came to faith in Christ. She died when I was thirteen, but I never forgot her faith.

Recently I babysat my granddaughter while her parents went out on a "date night." My wife was out of town, so it was just Stella and Papa. We played together. I let her pick out what we would have for supper: hot dogs, macaroni and cheese, and peas. (Yes, she chose peas!) We ate sitting on the living room floor while watching cartoons together. At one point I took her outside to look at the stars; our home is in the country, so the skies are dark and the stars are bright. I pointed out various constellations and reminded her that her name, Stella, means "star." We came back inside, had cookies and ice cream, read books, and then, two hours after her official bedtime, I put her to bed (the joy of being a grandparent!).

As I lay down with her to put her to sleep, I said to her, "Stella, I want to tell you about something that is really important to Papa." She looked at me attentively. I asked, "Do you remember the stars?" She nodded. "Do you know that Someone made them all and calls them all by name? That someone is God. He made trees and rabbits and puppies and little girls. We can't see him, but he's all around us. And Stella, he loves you. When Mimi and Papa pray, we are talking to him. And do you know what we say to him when we pray? We say thank you." And with that, Stella and I prayed together.

I think that's what Moses was saying in Deuteronomy. Intentionally sharing and living your faith is crucial so that your children and grandchildren know what you believe and how it shapes your life and so that they see a real and authentic faith in you.

Remember the Lord

Moses' concern was not just for future generations; he was worried that the generation standing before him might forget or lose their own faith once they entered the Promised Land. Fifteen times in Deuteronomy he tells the Israelites to remember or not to forget. You can hear his concern clearly in this text from chapter 8:

> When you eat, get full, build nice houses, and settle down, and when your herds and your flocks are growing large, your silver and gold are multiplying, and everything you have is thriving, don't become arrogant, forgetting the LORD your God:
>
> > the one who rescued you from Egypt, from the house of slavery.…
>
> Don't think to yourself, My own strength and abilities have produced all this prosperity for me. Remember the LORD your God! He's the one who gives you the strength to be prosperous.
>
> > (Deuteronomy 8:12-14, 17-18)

Old Testament scholar Walter Brueggemann wrote in his book *Spirituality of the Psalms* about the seasons of life that Israel seemed to cycle through regularly, seasons that we recognize in our own lives.[7] He described these seasons as orientation, disorientation, and reorientation. Orientation is when things are going well—so well, in fact, that over time it's easy to forget God. In these seasons we experience the words to the old hymn: "Prone to wander, Lord, I feel it, prone to leave the God I love."[8] Disorientation is when we wander from God and feel fear, anxiety, and pain. When Israel wandered from God she made poor choices, uninformed by her faith. God's hand of protection was no longer with her. The nation would find itself in trouble, and enemies would gain the upper hand. In these seasons Israel would cry out to God, asking for help and forgiveness. And God, who is rich in mercy, would rescue Israel, healing, forgiving, and restoring her. These seasons Brueggemann referred to as reorientation. In these moments after receiving forgiveness and restoration we experience ecstatic joy and feelings of gratitude and hope. Over time, however, reorientation gives way to orientation, which can lead to straying and disorientation all over again. In a sense Israel's story, and our story, can be told in the light of this ever-repeating cycle.

The story of the Exodus had already seen these cycles. The cycles started with disorientation when the Israelites were slaves in Egypt. Intense joy and gratitude of reorientation followed when

God delivered the Israelites from Pharaoh. These feelings gave way to orientation, and then seasons when the people, forgetting God's mighty acts of deliverance, began to grumble and complain, leading once more to disorientation. In their distress, the people would cry out to God once more, and God would always take them back again.

We can see Deuteronomy's timelessness when we recognize that it's not just Israel's story; it's our story. We're all "prone to wander... prone to leave the God I love."[9]

Much of Deuteronomy recounts portions of the Law, but it includes one verse, one command, that stands above all the rest. Faithful Jews place this verse in a mezuzah and hang it on the doorpost of their home. They recite the verse every morning when they awaken and every night before going to sleep. They hope to have the presence of mind to recite it before taking their final breath:

> Israel, listen! Our God is the LORD! Only the LORD!

> Love the LORD your God with all your heart, all your being, and all your strength.
>
> (Deuteronomy 6:4-5)

This command is repeated multiple times in Deuteronomy as the essence of what God seeks from his people. Jesus described this as the first and most important commandment, then added Leviticus 19:18, as a corollary to it: "You must love your neighbor as yourself." These two, Jesus said, summarize all the Law and the Prophets.

The words are simple, but they reflect a deep sense of God's purpose in creating humankind.

I want to include here a couple of lengthier passages from Deuteronomy, as they capture in such beautiful ways the tone and content of the book. In Deuteronomy 10, Moses says to the people,

So now, O Israel, what does the LORD your God require of you? Only to fear the LORD your God, to walk in all his ways, to love him, to serve the LORD your God with all your heart and with all your soul, and to keep the commandments of the LORD your God and his decrees that I am commanding you today, for your own well-being. Although heaven and the heaven of heavens belong to the LORD your God, the earth with all that is in it, yet the LORD set his heart in love on your ancestors alone and chose you, their descendants after them, out of all the peoples, as it is today. Circumcise, then, the foreskin of your heart, and do not be stubborn any longer. For the LORD your God is God of gods and LORD of lords, the great God, mighty and awesome, who is not partial and takes no bribe, who executes justice for the orphan and the widow, and who loves the strangers, providing them food and clothing. You shall also love the stranger, for you were strangers in the land of Egypt. You shall fear the LORD your God; him alone you shall worship; to him you shall hold fast, and by his name you shall swear. He is your praise; he is your God, who has done for you these great and awesome things that your own eyes have seen. Your ancestors went down to Egypt seventy persons; and now the LORD your God has made you as numerous as the stars in heaven.

(Deuteronomy 10:12-22 NRSV)

In Deuteronomy 11, Moses once again pleads with the people not to forget the Lord and his commands, and to teach their children these things:

If you will only heed his every commandment that I am commanding you today—loving the LORD your God, and serving him with all your heart and with all your soul— then he will give the rain for your land in its season, the early rain

and the later rain, and you will gather in your grain, your
wine, and your oil; and he will give grass in your fields for
your livestock, and you will eat your fill. Take care, or you
will be seduced into turning away, serving other gods and
worshiping them, for then the anger of the LORD will be
kindled against you and he will shut up the heavens, so that
there will be no rain and the land will yield no fruit; then
you will perish quickly off the good land that the LORD is
giving you.

You shall put these words of mine in your heart and soul, and
you shall bind them as a sign on your hand, and fix them as
an emblem on your forehead. Teach them to your children,
talking about them when you are at home and when you are
away, when you lie down and when you rise. Write them on
the doorposts of your house and on your gates, so that your
days and the days of your children may be multiplied in the
land that the LORD swore to your ancestors to give them, as
long as the heavens are above the earth.

(Deuteronomy 11:13-21 NRSV)

These two passages summarize not only Deuteronomy, but the
entirety of the Torah.

In Deuteronomy 12–26, Moses recites various provisions from
the Law that are previously found in Exodus, Leviticus, and Numbers.
Finally the book moves to what seems to have been a standard part
of ancient vassal treaties, a set of blessings and curses demonstrating
the benefits of remaining faithful to the treaty or covenant and the
punishments or curses that would come if the people broke the
covenant. Chapters 27, 28, and 29 capture the blessings and curses:
blessings of life lived for God and curses that come when God's
people turn away.

Following these chapters, we reach Moses' dramatic conclusion to his farewell discourse.

> I have set before you life and death, blessings and curses.
> Choose life so that you and your descendants may live, loving
> the LORD your God, obeying him, and holding fast to him;
> for that means life to you.
>
> (Deuteronomy 30:19-20 NRSV)

These words are as powerful today as they were when they were first uttered. Choose life by loving the Lord and obeying and holding fast to him.

The Promised Land

Following this dramatic challenge, Moses formally appointed Joshua as his successor. Then Moses turned from the people and walked up Mount Nebo, much as he had done nearly forty years earlier at Mount Sinai.

Mount Nebo rises 2,680 feet above sea level and is ten miles from where the Jordan River flows into the Dead Sea. Atop the mountain now sits a Franciscan Church, recently renovated and expanded. In 1932 the Franciscans acquired the site from a local Bedouin tribe after the foundations and mosaic tile floors of a fourth-century church were found there.

As with each site on our journey in the footsteps of Moses, we can't be certain that this mountain is the historic Mount Nebo. We do know that for at least 1,700 years, pilgrims have been going there to remember Moses' death and to catch a glimpse of the Promised Land as he may have seen it before he died.[10]

Memorial Church of Moses, Mount Nebo. Inset: Serpentine cross sculpture, "Brazen Serpent Monument" by Giovanni Fantoni, Mount Nebo

As I stood on Mount Nebo, looking out over the plains of Moab, the Jordan River Valley, and beyond that to the Holy Land, a couple of busloads of people arrived. They quickly dashed from place to place snapping pictures. I wanted to plead with them to stop for a moment simply to stand there and take it all in—to picture the aged Moses, leaning on his staff, reflecting upon his life and journey. Deuteronomy 34 describes what this scene must have been like:

> Then Moses hiked up from the Moabite plains to Mount Nebo, the peak of the Pisgah slope, which faces Jericho. The LORD showed him the whole land: the Gilead region as far as Dan's territory; all the parts belonging to Naphtali along with the land of Ephraim and Manasseh, as well as the entirety of Judah as far as the Mediterranean Sea; also the arid southern

plain, and the plain—including the Jericho Valley, Palm City—as far as Zoar.

Then the LORD said to Moses: "This is the land that I swore to Abraham, Isaac, and Jacob when I promised: 'I will give it to your descendants.'"

(Deuteronomy 34:1-4)

From this location, with his naked eyes, Moses could not have seen all these places. He would have seen as far as Jericho, the Dead Sea, the Jordan River Valley, and the Judean countryside but not beyond. In that moment God, in his tenderness and mercy, allowed Moses to see the Promised Land in his mind's eye, to view what he had spent forty years dreaming of and casting a vision for—a land flowing with milk and honey. Though Moses did not enter the land, God allowed him to "see" it before he died.

Moses had spent forty years telling the Israelites about the Promised Land. We can certainly say that Moses' vision of the land and his ability to cast that vision for the Israelites provides a lesson in leadership. I've heard pastor Bill Hybels say, "The job of a leader is to take people from here to there." "Here" is the world as it is; "there" is a better future, a "preferred picture of the future" as vision is so often defined.

When the Israelites complained about the lack of food and water in the wilderness and wanted to return to Egypt, Moses would say, "Let me tell you about a land flowing with milk and honey, where you will live and your children will grow up free."

But as Moses stood there on the top of Mount Nebo, looking over Canaan, he knew that the Promised Land wasn't just the roughly eight thousand square miles that make up the modern state

View of Promised Land from Mt. Nebo

of Israel. The Promised Land was an ideal, a place where God's will is done, a taste of heaven on earth. If the people lived according to God's commands, it would mean a return to paradise where humans didn't kill or hurt one another, where people loved their neighbors, where justice and mercy reigned. Jesus, too, knew that the Promised Land wasn't a plot of ground. He spoke of it as the Kingdom of God.

All of us need a compelling vision of the Promised Land. The task of leaders is to help us see what we cannot see and move us to give ourselves in pursuit of a vision bigger than ourselves. That vision is meant to drive us, shape us, and move us to accept sacrifice and hardship along the way in pursuit of a better "there." In modern times, one of the most compelling pictures of the Promised Land was the dream of Dr. Martin Luther King, Jr.

On the night before he was shot to death on the balcony of the Lorraine Motel in Memphis, Dr. King preached at the Mason Temple Church of God. He had come to Memphis to stand with sanitation workers in their quest for a living wage.

That night King wasn't feeling well, but he didn't want to disappoint the crowds who had gathered to hear him. As usual there had been death threats. As he preached he began by recounting what had brought him to Memphis and the journey he had taken during the civil rights movement. He laid out a strategy to effect change. He unpacked the parable of the good Samaritan. The sermon is a masterpiece. I encourage you to read it. As Deuteronomy was for Moses, this sermon in Memphis would be King's final testimony.

You'll recall that King, as he ended his sermon, preaching with all the fire and conviction he could muster, drew upon the story of Moses ascending Mount Nebo. He told his followers that God had allowed him to go up to the mountain and see the Promised Land. He noted, "I may not get there with you. But I want you to know tonight that we, as a people, will get to the promised land!"[11]

Let me ask you: What is your Promised Land? What is the vision that drives you, the end to which your whole life is progressing? What is, for you, the pearl of great price? Is it a certain income level? a house? a kind of car? the corner office at work? Maybe it's travel and trips? But none of these rises to the level of being a compelling vision for your life. Moses' vision of the Promised Land was ultimately not about a parcel of ground, but about a people who would love the Lord, hold fast to him, and obey his commands, and who would love their neighbors as they loved themselves.

The Death of Moses

Deuteronomy tells us,

> Then Moses, the servant of the LORD, died there in the land
> of Moab, at the LORD's command. He was buried in a valley
> in the land of Moab, opposite Beth-peor, but no one knows
> his burial place to this day. Moses was one hundred twenty
> years old when he died; his sight was unimpaired and his
> vigor had not abated. The Israelites wept for Moses in the
> plains of Moab thirty days; then the period of mourning for
> Moses was ended.
>
> (Deuteronomy 34:5-8 NRSV)

On the day that he died, I believe Moses finally did set foot in
the Promised Land, welcomed by his parents and by the patriarchs
and saints who had gone before him. He was also welcomed by the
God who had saved him as a child, placed a concern for the Israelite
slaves on his heart as a young man, called him from the burning bush
at age eighty, and walked with him every day as he sought to lead the
Israelites in the years since. This was the land flowing with milk and
honey, of which Canaan was just a dim reflection.

I'll give the writer of Deuteronomy the final words in telling
Moses' story.

> Never since has there arisen a prophet in Israel like Moses,
> whom the LORD knew face to face. He was unequaled for all
> the signs and wonders that the LORD sent him to perform in
> the land of Egypt, against Pharaoh and all his servants and his
> entire land, and for all the mighty deeds and all the terrifying
> displays of power that Moses performed in the sight of all
> Israel.
>
> (Deuteronomy 34:10-12 NRSV)

NOTES

Introduction

1. Martin Luther King Jr., "I See the Promised Land," in *A Testament of Hope*, ed. James M. Washington (San Francisco: HarperOne, 1991), 286.

2. One of the best-known theories concerning the composition of the Torah is called the Documentary Hypothesis. This hypothesis suggests there were four primary sources for the material in the Torah, sources that were composed over a period of 500 years or more and eventually compiled and redacted into the Torah we have today. Over the last 150 years, the Documentary Hypothesis has been debated, criticized, and modified. Some conservatives reject it completely. Most mainline scholars accept the basic assumption that Moses did not write most of the Torah and that it is composed of material from various sources written over hundreds of years.

3. The terms *minimalist* and *maximalist* have a range of meaning. The views of some maximalists would be akin to my own views described

in this paragraph and the following, while other maximalists would be what are often referred to as inerrantists, biblicists, or literalists, believing that everything in the Moses story happened exactly as it is recorded in the Old Testament accounts. For an excellent interview with a Reform Jewish scholar who holds a view between the minimalists and maximalists, see the interview with Richard Elliott Friedman at http://www.reformjudaism.org/exodus-not-fiction.

Chapter 1

1. For example, two hundred years after the Great Pyramid was built, and not far from it, Pharaoh Unas would build his pyramid. Lining the walls of his burial chamber, and the other chambers inside the pyramid, were texts guiding the pharaoh on his final journey not only to eternal life but to divinity. From the time of Unas on, the burial chambers of the pyramids appear to have been engraved with what have become known as "pyramid texts," consisting of spells and guides that later became the basis for the Egyptian Book of the Dead.

2. If Moses was born in 1350 B.C., his formative years would have been during the early reign of Amenhotep IV, who later built a new capital (Akhetaten, later known as Amarna) and changed his name to Akhenaten. This pharaoh led a radical religious revolution favoring a quasi-monotheism—the worship of Aten (portrayed as the sun) over against all other Egyptian gods—in essence saying that the Egyptian people were to have no other gods before Aten. I can't help but wonder if this period prepared the way for Moses, years later, to embrace monotheism himself. After Akhenaten's death in 1334 B.C., the capital returned to Thebes, and Egypt returned to the worship of the broader pantheon of Egyptian gods. By that time Moses would have been sixteen, and the royal family would have been led by King Tutankhamun (who, thanks to the discovery of his nearly intact burial chambers in 1924, is well known to us as King Tut).

3. Ahmose I destroyed the Hyksos capital located in the Delta sometime after 1539 B.C. but before a proposed early date for the birth of Moses. Another capital city would not be built there until after 1295 B.C., long after a late date for Moses' birth.

4. Again, if we ascribe a late date for Moses, he may have lived in Akhetaten from 1343 B.C. when it became the new capital until the death of Akhenaten in 1334 B.C. Before and after those dates, however, he would have lived in Thebes. Again, bear in mind as noted previously, even Moses' age as described in Scripture might be more symbolic than literal.

5. This account is similar to the Sumerian story of Sargon the Great, who lived about a thousand years before Moses. He too was placed by his mother in a basket that served as a boat, and he floated down the river. He was found, though in his case by a man, a gardener. Some believe Moses' story was borrowed from Sargon's. Others wonder if the borrowing didn't work the other way around, given that the earliest record of Sargon's story is from about seven hundred years before Christ, some six hundred years after the birth of Moses.

6. I mention four women: Jochebed and Pharaoh's daughter, along with Shiphrah and Puah. I believe the writer of Exodus intends for us to imagine Shiphrah and Puah as still being midwives when Moses was born, though it is possible they only served in the time prior to his birth.

Chapter 2

1. In the Book of Exodus, the word *Hebrew* is used interchangeably with the word *Israelite*. In the ancient world, *Hebrew* may have been used to describe various nomadic peoples of Semitic descent.

2. The official name of the monastery is the "Sacred Monastery of the God-Trodden Mount Sinai."

3. There is a tradition of biblical figures meeting their wives at wells. Women's responsibilities included drawing water, so if a man wanted to meet a woman, the well seemed a good place. (I'm reminded that in some circles even today, "watering hole" and "well" are euphemisms for bars where single people go to meet.) In Scripture, Abraham's servant went in search of a wife for Isaac and met Rebekah at a well (Genesis 24:10-15). Jacob met his wife Rachel at a well as she came to water the flock (Genesis 29:1-14).. These stories also form an interesting backdrop for John 4, in which Jesus met a woman at "Jacob's well" and asked her for a drink; the woman, we are told, had been married and divorced four times and was living with a man who was not her husband.

4. Isabelle Khoo, "Celebrities You Wouldn't Believe Were Bullied In School," *The Huffington Post Canada*, published October 2, 2015, accessed January 5, 2017, http://www.huffingtonpost.ca /2015/10/02/celebrities-who-were-bullied_n_8234100.html.

5. Elsewhere Zipporah's father is called Jethro. Some believe Reuel and Jethro were the same man; others suggest they were two separate men.

6. The number of sons Moses had at this point is open to interpretation. Exodus 2:22 only mentions one son, Gershom. Exodus 4:20 speaks of "his wife and his children." And Exodus 18:3-4 names two sons, Gershom and Eliezer, but Eliezer was never mentioned prior to the burning bush. For purposes of this narrative we will assume two sons.

7. Jethro is portrayed in a positive light in Exodus, despite his likely polytheism. But later, in the Book of Numbers, Moses commanded the Israelite army to kill all the men and boys in Midian. This was in response to a plot by the Midianite leaders to coax the Israelite men to serve one of their gods, Baal of Peor, by offering the Israelite men some of their women. The story begins in Numbers 25 but climaxes in Numbers 31, one of the most disturbing stories in the Torah. God commands Moses to go to war with Midian and to exact retribution

from them. Moses commands the Israelite army, in God's name, to kill every man, every male child, and all the women who were not virgins. It is possible that only certain tribes of the Midianites were attacked, specifically those who had sought to undermine Israel. For reflections on how to make sense of these kinds of violent passages in the Bible, see "The Violence of God" in my book *Making Sense of the Bible*, San Francisco: HarperOne, 2014).

8. In various Middle Eastern cultures it is an insult to cross your legs in a way that shows the bottom of your shoes. And the ultimate insult is to step on someone using your shoe, to hit someone with the bottom of your shoe, or to throw a shoe at someone. (You may recall that Iraqi journalist Muntazer al-Zaidi made international news in 2008 when he threw a shoe at then-President George W. Bush.)

9. One of the interesting items on display in the monastery is a copy of a letter said to have been dictated by Muhammad in A.D. 626, granting protection to the monastery as well as broad, sweeping protections for Christians. Its words seem particularly pertinent in our time of ongoing religious conflict.

10. *Yahweh* is sometimes pronounced Jehovah, using the same four consonants but supplying different vowel sounds. Most scholars consider this to be a mispronunciation, the result of Jewish scribes adding vowel "points" to the word YHWH that were intended to lead readers to say the word *Adonai* whenever YHWH appears in Scripture. (*Adonai* is the common word for Lord.) When the vowel sounds from Adonai are combined with the consonants of YHWH, they result in the word *Jehovah*.

Chapter 3

1. Exodus 4:18-24 raises interesting questions for the reader and likely supports the idea that there were various sources for the material in the Torah that were edited together much later. Here are a few things to note in this section of Scripture: God had already called Moses

to go to Egypt, and he had already agreed, yet verse 19 sounds like a new calling from God for Moses to return to Egypt. Verse 20 implies that Moses had small children who would sit on the donkey with their mother, yet up to this point in the story only one child has been mentioned. Then verse 24 again seems to indicate there was only one son. These are just a few small examples of many places throughout the Torah where it appears as though different chronologies and accounts were brought together to form the story as we have it today.

2. Jeffrey M. Cohen, "*Hatan Damim* – The Bridegroom of Blood," *Jewish Bible Quarterly 33*, no. 2 (April–June 2005): na.

3. Conservative scholars rightly note that the Bible does from time to time use the place names of cities from later periods in recounting events that occurred in earlier times, so references to a city named after Ramesses II is not a definitive argument for the later dating approach.

4. Rabbi Jonathan Sacks, *Covenant & Conversation Exodus: The Book of Redemption* (New Milford, CT: Maggid Books, 2010), 260.

5. There was not one Book of the Dead; in various periods different "spells" were included, and the book was personalized for each individual.

6. Numbers 33:4 mentions that it was only the firstborn males that were put to death. My estimate is based upon a total population of 2.9 million suggested by Butzler in his *Early Hydraulic Civilization* (Chicago: University of Chicago Press, 1976), 84, table 4. Subtracting Israelite slaves, and assuming an average family size of six surviving children, with half of the firstborn in these families being females, I land at an estimate of, at minimum, 100,000 firstborn males who died. The number could have been much higher.

7. The Black Death, caused by the *Yersinia pestis* bacterium, is known as bubonic plague. It produces boils on the skin and is transmitted by fleas, which reminds us of the third plague, the plague of the small

biting insects, usually translated as lice. In the case of bubonic plague, 30 percent or more of those afflicted can, without proper treatment, die within ten days. The death toll from the Black Death or bubonic plague ranges in estimates from fifty million to two hundred million.

8. The Last Supper was a Passover Seder in Matthew, Mark, and Luke. In John the timing is different, as the author seeks to emphasize that Jesus was the Passover lamb that was slain. Hence, in John's Gospel, Jesus is crucified earlier, at the hour when the Passover lambs were slaughtered in preparation for the Passover Seder.

9. The city of Ismalia is located mostly on the north shore of Lake Timsah. Built in 1862–63 in part as a base for the construction of the Suez Canal and its thousands of forced laborers, the city was named after Ismail Pasha, the grandson of Muhammed Ali Pasha, founder of modern Egypt, who built a palace there. The canal runs along, and is a part of, the east side of the lake. The city is the midpoint of the Suez Canal, between the Mediterranean Sea and the Gulf of Suez on the Red Sea. Small "mom and pop" hotels dot the landscape along the western side of the lake, along with beautiful new luxury homes.

Chapter 4

1. The same idea is found in Revelation 1:6, 5:10, and 20:6.

2. Pilgrims who leave early enough arrive at the top of Mount Sinai just before dawn and can witness the sunrise from there. Because our crew had been exhausted after multiple days of filming, we had begun our journey only an hour before dawn, and as a result watched the sunrise from two-thirds of the way up the mountain, still a beautiful sight but nothing like the footage I've seen from the top. Because of a tight schedule, we came down the mountain early in order to catch our flight in the city of Sharm El Sheikh, leaving me anxious to make another trek to Egypt to explore the summit at sunrise.

3. Rabbi Lord Jonathan Sacks, "Yitro (5768) – A Holy Nation", *The Office of Rabbi Sacks,* January 26, 2008, http://rabbisacks.org /covenant-conversation-5768-yitro-a-holy-nation/.

4. "A Service of Christian Marriage," *The United Methodist Hymnal* (Nashville: The United Methodist Publishing House, 1989), 867.

5. Ben Dipietro, "Reader Poll: Wells Fargo Chosen as Scandal of the Year," *The Wall Street Journal*, December 38, 2016. http://blogs.wsj .com/riskandcompliance/2016/12/28/reader-poll.

6. Marc Fisher, John Woodrow Cox, and Peter Hermann, "Pizzagate: From rumor, to hashtag, to gunfire in D.C.," *The Washington Post*, December 6, 2016. https://www.washingtonpost.com/local/ pizzagate-from-rumor-to-hashtag-to-gunfire-in-dc/2016/12 /06/4c7def50-bbd4-11e6-94ac-3d324840106c_story.html ?utm_term=.810301c6eef5.

7. Note that Catholics and Lutherans divide this into two commandments, even as they combine what I've listed as the first two commandments.

Chapter 5

1. The reference to the Philistines here is one among many clues that the story of the Exodus was written long after the time of Moses. Most scholars believe the Philistines didn't arrive in this region until decades after the Exodus. A more likely reason for avoiding the short route was that the Egyptians had fortresses along the way, and by going south the Israelites would have avoided these fortresses. The point of the text is the same either way: God led the Israelites away from potential battles, recognizing that the Israelites might well have become so fearful or discouraged that they would have opted to return to Egypt—something they threatened to do multiple times anyway, as we will see in this chapter.

2. See Antti Laato's brief but excellent summary of how to translate the Hebrew word *kapporet* at http://journal.fi/store/article/view /41590.

3. See in Hebrews 9 a description of how, for the early Christians, this mercy seat and the priests' offering prefigured what Jesus came to do by his death. When Matthew 27:51 mentions the tearing of the veil in the Temple at Jesus' death, Scripture is alluding to the same idea pointed to by the writer of Hebrews.

4. "How Great Thou Art," *The United Methodist Hymnal*, 77.

5. E. H. Palmer, *The Desert of the Exodus: Journeys on Foot in the Wilderness of the Forty Years' Wanderings* (Cambridge, 1871) is in the public domain and available for free download. Download the PDF for the best reading experience.

6. From the introduction to W. F. Hume, *The Topography and Geology of the Peninsula of Sinai* (Cairo, National Printing Department, 1906), 11. This fascinating volume is also available as a free download.

7. There are two locations most often identified as Kadesh Barnea. Most mainline scholars identify the place as located in a long valley with an oasis that grows a wide variety of fruit and dates in the Negev Desert. Some others suggest that Kadesh is an ancient name for the area later known as Petra in Jordan. Reading Numbers and Deuteronomy can be a bit confusing if one is trying to discern precisely when and where the Israelites were during the thirty-eight years. In part, this is likely due to the various sources for this material that have been edited together. But my reading of the text is that they spent most of this time at Kadesh Barnea.

8. Andrew Dugan and Frank Newport, "Americans Rate JFK as Top Modern President," Gallup.com, November 15, 2013. http://www .gallup.com/poll/165902/americans-rate-jfk-top-modern-president .aspx.

9. National Parks Service, *Mount Rushmore South Dakota National Memorial Frequently Asked Questions*, accessed January 5, 2017, https://www.nps.gov/moru/faqs.htm.

10. U.S. Department of the Interior, National Parks Service, *Impacts of Visitor Spending on the Local Economy: Mount Rushmore National Memorial 2013*, by Philip S. Cook, Natural Resource Report NPS /NRSS/EQD/NRR—2014/796 (Natural Resource Stewardship and Science, Fort Collins, Co, 2014), https://irma.nps.gov /DataStore/DownloadFile/494891.

Chapter 6

1. I would direct the reader to "God's Violence in the Old Testament," a chapter in my book *Making Sense of the Bible* (HarperOne, 2014).

2. There has been a great deal of discussion among scholars about these vassal treaties or suzerainty treaties and how closely Deuteronomy parallels their form. Multiple examples from the Hittites and the Assyrians point to the idea that the treaty in its basic outline was familiar across cultures in the ancient Near East.

3. As this book is not a commentary, I've only given a nod to the scholarly debate about the composition and dating of the five books that constitute the Pentateuch or Torah. When it comes to Deuteronomy, many mainline scholars believe the book was written long after the time of Moses—in the seventh, sixth, or even fifth century B.C.—and was drawn from the traditions and stories that make up the books of Exodus, Leviticus, and Numbers to create a kind of "Reader's Digest" version of that story, placed on the lips of Moses. By contrast, many conservative scholars see Deuteronomy as being written by Moses or a scribe contemporaneous with Moses and reflecting the form of a vassal treaty dating to the time of Moses.

4. James C. Vanderkam, *The Dead Sea Scrolls and the Bible* (Grand Rapids, MI: Eerdmans, 2012), 3.

5.   This phrase, though perhaps not coined by Ronald Reagan, was first
      popularized by him in a speech to the Phoenix, Arizona Chamber
      of Commerce, March 30, 1961, https://archive.org/details
      /RonaldReagan-EncroachingControl. In the speech he noted that
      not faith but freedom, "is never more than one generation away from
      extinction. We didn't pass it on to our children in the bloodstream.
      The only way they can inherit the freedom we have known is if we
      fight for it, protect it, defend it and then hand it to them with the
      well thought lessons of how they in their lifetime must do the same.
      And if you and I don't do this, then you and I may well spend our
      sunset years telling our children and our children's children what it
      once was like in America when men were free." I believe the speech
      captures the same urgency and sentiment that Moses felt about his
      faith.

6.   Haydn Shaw, *Generational IQ : Christianity Isn't Dying, Millennials
      Aren't the Problem, and the Future Is Bright*, (Carol Stream, IL:
      Tyndale House, 2015), 189–191.

7.   Walter Brueggemann, *Spirituality of the Psalms* (Minneapolis:
      Augsburg Fortress, 2002).

8.   "Come, Thou Font of Every Blessing," *The United Methodist Hymnal*,
      400.

9.   Ibid.

10.   In 2 Maccabees 2:4-7, a book in the Pharisaic tradition that was
      written long after the time of either Moses or Jeremiah, we read that
      when the Babylonians came to destroy Jerusalem, Jeremiah took
      the Ark of the Covenant to Mount Nebo and hid it in a cave there,
      sealing it until the day when God would restore Israel.

11.   Martin Luther King Jr., "I See the Promised Land," in *A Testament of
      Hope*, 286

IMAGE CREDITS

Unless noted otherwise, photos courtesy of Adam Hamilton and Danielle Hamilton Slate.

Images pages 8, 20, and 44 courtesy of Peter Hermes Furian/Shutterstock.com.

Image page 24 courtesy of iStock.com/Peter Hermes Furian.

Images pages 70, 102, 128, 138, and 152 courtesy of Abingdon Press.

Image page 61 courtesy of Mildax /Shutterstock.com.

Image page 77 was photographed in 1889 by the German Egyptologist Emil Brugsch (1842-1930) and is now in the public domain.

Image page 97 courtesy of Evannovostro/Shutterstock.com.

Illustration page 134 by Ken Strickland.

Image page 143 from *Satellite Bible Atlas* by William Schlegel, courtesy of BiblePlaces.com.

Image page 150 courtesy of Todd Bolen/BiblePlaces.com.

Image page 156 courtesy of iStock.com/cinoby.

FOR FURTHER READING

Moses

Buber, Martin. *Moses: The Revelation and the Covenant.*
Amherst, NY: Humanity, 1998.

Martin Buber was a twentieth-century Jewish philosopher.
Though most well known and influential for his philo-
sophical works, he also had a deep interest in the Bible and
illuminating its meaning.

Coats, George W. *Moses: Heroic Man, Man of God. Journal*
for the Study of the Old Testament Supplement Series 57.
Sheffield: JSOT Press, 1988.

George Coats was a Professor of Old Testament at Lexington
Theological Seminary. The author of several books on

Genesis and Exodus, Coats has sought to illuminate biblical traditions surrounding Moses to understand better their development and influence.

The Exodus

Dozeman, Thomas B. *Exodus. Eerdmans Critical Commentary*. Grand Rapids: Eerdmans, 2009.

Thomas Dozeman is a Professor of Old Testament at United Theological Seminary. His thorough commentary on the Book of Exodus contains a wealth of insights into the structure of the book, how it may have been formed over time, and the major theological and literary themes within it.

Fretheim, Terence E. *Exodus. Interpretation: A Bible Commentary for Teaching and Preaching*. Louisville: Westminster John Knox Press, 1988.

This commentary on Exodus illuminates the theology of the book, with provocative insights that make Exodus come to life for people in today's world. Terence Fretheim is the Elva B. Lovell Professor Emeritus of Old Testament at Luther Theological Seminary.

Meyers, Carol. *Exodus. New Cambridge Bible Commentary*. New York: Cambridge University Press, 2005.

Carol Meyers is the Mary Grace Wilson Professor of Religion at Duke University. Her commentary sees Exodus as a cultural document of ancient Israel, and it contains historical, archaeological, and literary insights to help readers understand it more deeply.

Sarna, Nahum M. *Exploring Exodus: The Heritage of Biblical Israel.* New York: Schocken, 1986.

Nahum Sarna was a Professor of Biblical Studies at Brandeis University. The author of several books on Genesis and Exodus, Sarna offers in this book a detailed yet accessible exploration of Exodus in light of history and archaeology.

The Pentateuch

Alter, Robert. *The Five Books of Moses: A Translation with Commentary.* New York: Norton, 2004.

Robert Alter is the Class of 1937 Professor of Hebrew and Comparative Literature at the University of California, Berkeley. He has made important contributions to the study of the Hebrew Bible as literature, illuminating themes, motifs, and conventions that help us understand the Bible more deeply. This volume contains his own translation of Genesis, Exodus, Leviticus, Numbers, and Deuteronomy, with commentary presenting his insights into each book.

Blenkinsopp, Joseph. *The Pentateuch: An Introduction to the First Five Books of the Bible.* Anchor Yale Bible Reference Library. New Haven, CT: Yale University Press, 2000.

A standard overview of the first five books of the Bible, this book introduces readers to key issues in understanding the history behind the Pentateuch, how it developed over time, and how we can comprehend it today. Joseph Blenkinsopp is the John A. O'Brien Professor Emeritus of Biblical Studies at the University of Notre Dame.

Kaminsky, Joel S. and Joel N. Lohr. *The Torah: A Beginner's Guide.* Oneworld, 2011.

In this accessible overview of the Torah, the authors introduce the books of Genesis, Exodus, Leviticus, Numbers, and Deuteronomy while also offering theological insights into these books. A comparison of Jewish and Christian theological perspectives provides a rich reading experience and opportunities for discussion and engagement. Joel Kaminsky is the Morningstar Professor of Jewish Studies and Professor of Religion at Smith College. Joel Lohr is the Dean of Religious Life and associate professor at University of the Pacific.

The Bible and History

Coogan, Michael D., ed. *The Oxford History of the Biblical World.* Oxford: Oxford University Press, 1998.

This volume is a collection of essays about the history of biblical Israel and early Judaism and Christianity, helping readers understand each major historical period. Chapters by Wayne T. Pitard, Carol A. Redmount, and Lawrence E. Stager cover the time before, during, and after Israel's exodus from Egypt, as well as the emergence of Israel as a people.

Hoffmeier, James Karl. *Israel in Egypt: The Evidence for the Authenticity of the Exodus Tradition.* **New York: Oxford University Press, 1997.**

James Hoffmeier is a Professor of Old Testament and Ancient Near Eastern History and Archaeology. His book explores historical and archaeological evidence for the Israelites' exodus from Egypt, making the case for an authentic historical event underlying the biblical narrative.

Matthews, Victor H. and Don C. Benjamin. *Old Testament Parallels: Laws and Stories from the Ancient Near East.* **3d ed. New York: Paulist, 2006.**

This book contains translations of ancient texts relevant to the history underlying the Old Testament, including stories and documents that help illuminate the books of Exodus–Deuteronomy and the biblical story of Moses. It has helped many teachers introduce their students to the larger world in which the Bible came to be written. Victor Matthews is Dean of the College of Humanities and Public Affairs and Professor of Religious Studies at Missouri State University. Don Benjamin teaches Biblical and Near Eastern Studies at Arizona State University.

Other Commentaries

Anderson, Bernhard W. *Understanding the Old Testament.* **Abridged 4th ed. Upper Saddle River, NJ: Prentice-Hall, 1998.**

Bernhard W. Anderson was Professor of Old Testament Theology at Princeton Theological Seminary. Through this widely-used and much-loved textbook, he has introduced many students and pastors to the literature of the Old Testament.

Craigie, Peter C. The Book of Deuteronomy. New International Commentary on the Old Testament. Grand Rapids: Eerdmans, 1976.

Peter C. Craigie was academic vice president at the University of Calgary, Alberta, where he previously served as a professor of religious studies. His commentary on Deuteronomy explores the role of covenant as a key theme and highlights the book's relevance for people today.

Keck, Leander E., ed. The New Interpreter's Bible. Vol 1. Nashville: Abingdon Press, 1994.

The New Interpreter's Bible is a twelve-volume commentary on the whole Bible, with a particular focus on preaching, teaching, and theological study. In addition to commentary on the first three books of the Bible, the first volume also includes helpful introductions to the Old Testament and the Bible as a whole.

Miller, Patrick D. Deuteronomy. Interpretation: A Bible Commentary for Teaching and Preaching. Louisville: Westminster John Knox Press, 1990.

Patrick D. Miller is the Charles T. Haley Professor Emeritus of Old Testament Theology at Princeton Theological Seminary. In this important volume, Miller explores the Book of Deuteronomy with attention to the book's theology within its historical setting.

Walton, John H., ed. Zondervan Illustrated Bible Backgrounds Commentary. Vol. 1. Grand Rapids: Zondervan, 2009.

The Zondervan Illustrated Bible Background Commentary offers an introduction and verse-by-verse commentary for each biblical book, with key historical and archaeological information, illustrations, and photographs to help readers understand the world of the Bible. Volume 1 includes commentary on Genesis, Exodus, Leviticus, Numbers, and Deuteronomy.

ACKNOWLEDGMENTS

This book, the DVD designed to accompany it, the children's and youth studies, and the leader guide could not have happened without the amazing team at Abingdon Press. I am indebted to them. Thanks to Susan Salley, who is a constant source of encouragement and who dreams with me about these projects. Ron Kidd, my editor at Abingdon Press, takes the manuscript and works magic—raising questions, correcting my gaffs, and working hard to bring graphics and maps together into the finished product. Other team members all played important roles: Tim Cobb, Marcia Myatt, Selena Cunningham, Judith Pierson, Alan Vermilye, Camilla Myers, Tracey Craddock, Sonia Worsham, and others too numerous to mention.

I'm indebted to Dr. Brian Sigmon, editor at Abingdon Press, for carefully reading the manuscript with the eye of an Old Testament scholar and making suggestions for improvements Thank you, Brian! You were a great gift on this project.

Adam with Lee Rudeen, Bryan Rich, and James Ridgeway

As noted in the dedication, this project would not have happened without the support of James Ridgeway at Educational Opportunities Tours. EO sponsored the trip for myself and three team members, providing transportation, guides, lodging, and meals as well as a great deal of guidance as we planned for the trip to Egypt. James has a love for helping pastors and laypeople to explore the lands of the Bible, in the hope that they might see the Scriptures with fresh eyes, hear them with fresh ears, and that they might find their lives changed by the experience.

Our video crew consisted of Lee Rudeen, Lead Video Producer at The United Methodist Church of the Resurrection, and Resurrection member Bryan Rich, owner of Vessyl Media, who volunteered his time to film with us in Egypt. These guys worked harder than any two human beings should have to work, as we crossed Egypt and Jordan in the course of a week. The pace we kept to film the videos

Adam with Egyptian guides, Essam Mohamed Zeid and Ahmed Abd El Halim

was grueling, but they never stopped smiling. And Bryan, thanks for bringing the Osmo—it gave us some beautiful shots!

Lee Rudeen edited and produced the videos. I was astounded by the amount of time that went into producing these from the myriad video clips we filmed in Egypt and Jordan and then creating the studio shots and developing the maps and graphics. Lee, thank you for your dedication, your gifts, your commitment, and your love for this project. I am profoundly grateful for you. And thank you to Greg Hoeven for the great work on maps, animations, and graphics! Thanks, too, Kersee Meyer, for your help!

Special thanks to Yasser Mohamed Zeid, Director of Tourism with the Travellers Egypt Group, and Egyptologist Essam Mohamed Zeid, who was our guide during our journey through Egypt. Both Yasser and Essam were a tremendous blessing to us in providing support and guidance during the journey and made this a truly exceptional

Adam with his daughter, Danielle Hamilton Slate

experience. We are grateful for the Blue Bell Tour company in Jordan and our Jordanian guide, Michel Safer, who blessed us during our short stay in Jordan as we filmed at Mount Nebo.

It was a joy to have my daughter, Danielle Hamilton Slate, with me on the trip. Most of the photographs in this book were taken by her. Danielle, I'll always treasure taking this trip with you.

I want to thank the congregation at The United Methodist Church of the Resurrection. This book was first a sermon series in which I tested the ideas before starting to write the book. They graciously allowed me time to take this journey to Egypt.

Finally, I want to thank LaVon—my wife, companion, and best friend. I write these books on my own time, not on the church's time. What that really means is that I write them on her time. She gave up many days off, vacation days, and late nights so I could complete this manuscript. LaVon, thank you for your constant encouragement and love.

Educational Opportunities Tours

I would like to thank James Ridgeway and Educational Opportunities Tours (EO) for their support of the travel that made this book possible. They are an invaluable partner in the books I've written and small group videos I've prepared that take people to the lands of our faith and of the Bible.

Educational Opportunities has worked closely with me for more than fifteen years, sponsoring multiple trips to the Holy Land for my books *The Journey*, *The Way*, and *24 Hours That Changed the World*; continuing with my trip through the British Isles to follow in the footsteps of John Wesley that resulted in *Revival*; on my trip to Turkey, Greece, and Italy to trace the ministry of the Apostle Paul for *The Call*; and on this most recent trip to Egypt that resulted in the book you are now holding.

I encourage everyone to take at least one trip to the Holy Land in their lifetime. It will forever change how you read Scripture. Based on my experience with this book and the accompanying video, I encourage readers to consider a trip to Egypt as well.

–Adam Hamilton

**For more information,
go to www.eo.TravelWithUs.com.**

Adam Hamilton is senior pastor of The United Methodist Church of the Resurrection in the Kansas City area, cited as the most influential mainline church in America. Hamilton speaks across the U.S. each year on leadership and connecting with nonreligious and nominally religious people. A master at explaining questions of faith in a down-to-earth fashion, he is the author of many books including *Creed, Half Truths, John, The Journey, The Way, 24 Hours That Changed the World, Enough, When Christians Get it Wrong, Seeing Gray in a World of Black and White, Forgiveness, Love to Stay, Why?* and *Making Sense of the Bible.*

To learn more about Adam and follow his regular blog postings, visit www.AdamHamilton.org.

FAITHFUL
CHRISTMAS THROUGH
THE EYES OF JOSEPH

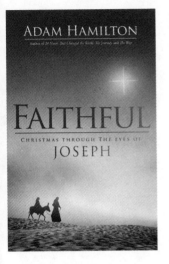

From his beginnings as a humble carpenter to his all-important role as the earthly father of Jesus Christ, Joseph's place in the nativity story is sometimes overlooked but contains valuable lessons for all of us. Join Adam Hamilton as he examines Christmas through the eyes of Joseph. Absent from much of the biblical narrative, Joseph never speaks a word, but his courageous actions were crucial to the birth of Christ and God's salvation plan for humanity.

As you read this book, you will understand how Joseph's story is much like our own. In life, we encounter circumstances that we would have never chosen for ourselves. At times it can be tempting just to walk away. Joseph provides us a great example of humbly obeying God even when we don't understand and faithfully moving forward in the strength that God provides.

Exchange your doubt for courage this Advent and Christmas season. Learn to accept and glorify God's will even when circumstances make it difficult to do so.

ISBN 978-1-5018-1408-2 *Hardcover with dust jacket /* 978-1-5018-1409-9 *eBook*

A small group leader guide, a DVD,
and study resources for children and youth are also available.

Abingdon Press™

Available wherever fine books are sold.
For more information about Adam Hamilton, visit www.AdamHamilton.org.